Erik's Story

Life in a Changing World

Frederik R-L Osborne

Willow Point Publishing

Erik's Story
Life in a Changing World

Frederik R-L Osborne

© 2024

Willow Point Publishing

Printed in USA

To Sheila
With Much Love

Contents

CHAPTER I

My First Memories

I was born in Auburn, NY, on October 18, 1926. My first memory is of the old house built by my great-grandparents, David Munson Osborne and Eliza Wright Osborne. He was prospering in the manufacture of farm machinery and built a large house at 99 South St. in Auburn in the Finger Lakes region between Syracuse and Rochester. According to family legend when the bills reached $100,000, he tore them up and stopped counting.

The house was a very solid brick structure with hardwood floors and oak doors. The first floor consisted of a study, a music room, a dining room, a library wing, my grandfather

(Thomas Mott Osborne)'s bedroom and, at the back of the house, the pantry, the kitchen, and the servants' dining room. The front hall opened onto a porch and to steps leading down to South Street. The side hall opened onto a porte-cochère. From the hall a passage led south to the library and what had been my grandfather's study. The library wing was built in 1913 by my grandfather to house his books. The house was heated with steam radiators and originally a wood furnace. Later, an oil furnace was installed. The stairs to the second floor had a solid oak banister with a statue on the newel post. The banister was very sturdy and perfect for sliding down, which my brothers, Richard and Devens, and I frequently did. Once I slid down just as my mother, Lillie Osborne, was leaning over the banister, showing my nurse a soup tureen. I hit the tureen, knocking it to the floor and smashing it. It is the only time I can remember my mother being really annoyed with me.

On the second floor there were bedrooms for my parents, my brothers, me, and my nurse. A door led to the servants' quarters at the back of the house. We had a cook, maids, and a gardener. On the third floor were two guest bedrooms and a ballroom with a reception room next to it. A dumbwaiter connected the ballroom to the first-floor pantry. A staircase led up to a cupola above, from which you could see most of Auburn. The house was typically Victorian, very solid brick with big rooms, high ceilings and dark oak woodwork.

There were on the property in addition to the main house a building my mother used as a studio, a large greenhouse, a two-story stable, a garden tool shed, a gazebo and a playhouse that my grandfather had bought for my cousins Hope and Olivia, daughters of my uncle David Osborne.

During the 1930s depression my father, Lithgow Osbone, had the main part of 99 torn down because of the expense of operating it—the servants that were needed to run it, the heating bill, the maintenance on it and the property taxes. I was terribly upset when it was torn down and announced firmly that I would rebuild it when I grew up. My father did not tear down the attached library, which had its own heating system. The library consisted of one vast and very handsome room, a smaller room, which had served as my grandfather's study, and a full cellar. When the main part of 99 was torn down we found that the furnace which heated the library was gas. However, there was no gas meter connected to it. Apparently, there were two gas companies in Auburn at one time and people would take both services and use the one that was cheaper that month. Clearly the second line was not switched off, no meter was attached, and we had free gas for a while. We had a meter added. We lived in 99 in the winter and moved to Willow Point, when our school ended.

Growing up in Auburn as an Osborne gave me a skewed idea of life. My great-grandfather had started a farm machinery factory which sold its equipment all over the world. The factory employed 5,000 people at its height in Auburn. After the business was sold, the family still owned the newspaper, the biggest hotel in town, and the first-run theater. As a child I can recall going to the theater and not buying a ticket. I would simply say Osborne and my friends and I would walk right in. The city hall and the Women's Educational and Industrial Union buildings had been given to the city by my family.

My great-grandmother, Eliza Wright Osborne,

was a very strong-minded woman. When the telephone company started to run a line next to her property on Fitch Avenue, she sent her gardeners out to fill up the postholes they were digging. The phone company went to court over the issue. The phone poles on Fitch Avenue are on the other side of the street.

CHAPTER 2

Willow Point Growing Up

The Willow Point house was originally the toll house for a plank road which ran from Auburn to Moravia. It was named Willow Point for the trees which grow on its shore. The house was purchased by my great-grandfather and his father-in-law, David Wright, in 1872 and converted into a summer home. It is located on the west shore of Owasco Lake, fourteen miles from Auburn. Owasco is one of the Finger Lakes and is ten miles long and three-quarters of a mile wide. The Willow Point house is one third of a mile from the nearest dwelling. A large lawn stretches from the front of the house down to the lake. A creek runs through the property. The train tracks were about ten feet behind the house and all conversation ceased when the trains went by. From time to time, we put pennies on the tracks to be squashed by trains. I have one I found years later.

The house had been mostly unoccupied from 1917 until 1922 when my grandfather gave it to my father. My father had moved back from Boston to Auburn to go to work for the *Auburn Citizen*. He bought adjoining land and built a driveway from the public road and constructed a garage. With this purchase the estate was about 40 acres. In the house he installed indoor plumbing and a furnace. A gasoline generator, lodged in a small nearby shed, provided direct electric current for lights in the house and for a pump which drew water from the lake. Ice was cut from the lake in the winter and stored in an icehouse attached to the main building. The hot water heater and the stove operated on bottled gas. Neither my electric train nor my lead molding machine would run on the direct current, nor most other electrical equipment for that matter. The gramophone had to be cranked. Telephone service was an eight-party line. Two rings meant the call was for us and one ring meant it was for the Harris Stewarts, who lived two points to the south. We knew most of the people on the line, as they lived in summer places along the lake shore. However, there were two farm families on the line as well. The wives liked to chat endlessly. If my mother wanted to make a call she would bring her knitting, take the phone off the hook, and listen and knit away until they finally hung up. Our staff consisted of a cook, a maid, a caretaker, and my nurse.

The railroad ran along the lake shore and through our property. In my childhood there were, I think, at least four trains a day. Two came in the morning, another came at five o'clock and the last one at ten or eleven at night. The five o'clock train brought the newspaper, which was tossed off as the train went by. In those days some of the comics were serial in nature and we would rush out to read what had befallen our favorite characters. The last train at night would come when we were safely in bed. The train would be headed south, and the noise would grow louder and louder, shaking the house and rattling the windows. For the first few nights it would wake me up. After that I would sleep through its passing. Willow Point was a flag stop, which meant that the train would stop to pick up passengers if a green and white flag signaled. My great-grandfather and grandfather had taken the train to Auburn on a regular basis. We used the passenger service only occasionally. Also, in the early days a lake steamer had chugged up and down the lake, stopping to pick up or let off passengers. Secretary of State William H. Seward had lived across the lake and there is a picture of him dining on the Willow Point front porch. Ted Case, who had invented talking motion pictures, lived on the next point. The soundtrack is called that because Ted Case thought it looked like the railroad tracks which ran through his property.

The trains finally stopped running in the 1970s and, in the course of time, the rails were removed, and the right-of-way land sold to the adjoining property owners. My father hired a landscaper to remove the railroad bed behind the house, giving us a view of the glen. When I inherited the house, I dug up all the ties the railroad had left and made a road all the way to the south end of our property. It is a delightful private walking or jogging trail.

On the front lawn someone had planted an apple tree and a cherry tree together and they had grown up intertwined giving the impression of one tree with both apples and cherries.

The front porch included a peasant bed, which my parents had bought in Denmark during one of their trips. It is mostly enclosed for warmth and had been used by a whole Danish family. It had been painted brown when my parents bought it. It was beautifully repainted and decorated by my mother. She had her break-fast in the bed every morning and welcomed grandchildren to crawl in beside her.

With the arrival of commercial electric power an electric refrigerator was installed. As a result, the icehouse was converted into a studio for my mother. She had a kiln and a potter's wheel and made a variety of figurines, tiles, bowls, and vases. Unfortunately, the foundations rotted, and the room had to be torn down in 2015.

Life at Willow Point in the 1930s was idyllic. We swam, sailed, rowed, built dams in the brook, climbed the glen, and explored the woods. A series of tutors kept an eye on us. and there were the children of my parents' friends to play with. They lived on the other points along the lake. The cook, the maid and my nurse all came with us to the lake. One gardener took care of 99 and another gardener took care of Willow Point.

My father also had a secretary at the office.

I slept on one porch on the south side of the house and my brothers on an adjoining porch. My parents had a third sleeping porch at the front of the house. At the north end of the house there was a guest room and rooms for the maid and the cook. My nurse, Mrs. Sitser, slept in a room next to my porch. My mother, who liked to ride, kept her horse in what was originally the garage, part way up the hill. When we moved to the lake from 99, she would ride her horse out from town. Later the building was remodeled into a cottage and continues as such.

Several summers we had fawns as pets. Their mothers had been killed by automobiles and they had been rescued by the Conservation Department. They were kept in a large pen and given milk twice a day. When fall came, they went back to the Department and, I believe, were simply turned loose in the Adirondacks. It was fun watching them gambol and grow. They were quite unafraid of us, but they really did not make very good pets. I wondered from time to time how they were surviving in the woods, not having been brought up in the wild. One summer my father bought a 1920s

Chevrolet sedan for $25, and the tutor and I spent the summer taking it apart so that I would learn how cars worked. I did learn some things, but I was never a good mechanic.

The playhouse, which was at 99, was moved to the Point by my father. He located it to look down across the lake. He called it his Think House and used it as a study. Then it was later moved down next to the guest house as sleeping quarters for Sam and Christopher. Later it was used by my stepmother, Sally Tenney Osborne. It is still there, occupied by my niece Nina. For years smelt would come up the creek each spring to spawn, so many of them one could not see the bottom of the creek. We would net them and fry them whole, very tasty. Sadly, they no longer come up the creek.

CHAPTER 3
Going to School

In the fall of 1931, I went to kindergarten at the Logan School, a private day school on Genesee Street in Auburn. The school has since closed, and the building now houses the Cayuga Museum of History and Art. It was a small school, mainly serving the children of my parents' friends. I have few memories of it except for being teased by a little friend because I was wearing a Democratic donkey pin during the 1932 election. He suggested that I was a donkey too, which upset me at the time. During that election my father ran for Congress as a Democrat on a platform of repealing Prohibition, the 18th Amendment. When trick-or-treat children came to the house on Halloween I was assigned to give them an election card promoting my father's campaign.

I was told to tell them to tell their parents to vote for my father. It was my first involvement with politics. While Franklin Roosevelt won, my father did not.

In 1933 my father was appointed New York State Conservation Commissioner, and my parents rented a house at 54 South Swan St. in Albany not far from the State Office Building and the State Capitol. I lived there with them for four years until I went off to boarding school in the sixth grade. My older brothers, who were already in boarding school, never lived in Albany. Over Christmas vacation, when my brothers came home, we went to Auburn and stayed in houses my parents rented for the holidays. Later, sleeping quarters were fixed up at the 99 library and we stayed there. My parents lived in what had been the study and my brothers and I in a large room in the basement.

When my father went to work in Albany, I was sent to the Albany Academy for Boys, a private day school. I can remember very little about the school or who else attended it. There was nobody from the school near our house, so I played almost exclusively with Mary and Emily Warner, two girls from next door. Their father was Major John Warner, head of the New York State police. Their mother was a daughter of Al Smith, former NYS governor and Democratic presidential candidate in 1928. Our house was located a block from the State Office Building, where my father worked. The house was owned by the Warners and abutted their house. We shared a grubby backyard in which we played. The house was right on the street and looked out on a church across the way.

In 1935 the Conservation Department observed the 50th anniversary of its founding with a ceremony at Lake Placid, NY. Franklin Roosevelt, as a former New York State governor, came to the event. He and my grandfather had led a movement to oppose the influence of Tammany Hall Democrats and he knew the family. As a result, my father took the three of us to meet him. I really cannot remember much of the event except for clasping him by the hand.

In the summer we lived at the Point and my father stayed in Albany during the week. On weekends he was driven to Willow Point in a Cadillac provided for him by the State. It included license plate number 13 and a siren.

The siren was never used except when he arrived at the top of the Willow Point driveway. Then it was sounded to let my mother know he was home. The siren carried very well and all our neighbors at the south end of the lake would say to each other that Lithgow was home. He was driven by his chauffeur, Billy Walsh, a state employee. Billy was an ex-convict from Brooklyn, who had become a protégé of my grandfather. Billy had done prison time for killing the man who had killed his father. This was during World War One and Billy was in the army. He shipped out to France immediately after the killing. He was arrested upon landing in France, shipped back to the United States, tried, convicted, and sent to prison. Billy regularly drove me to school and picked me up at the end of the school day. He had a .32 Colt automatic pistol which he kept in the pocket of the door. I remember that he encouraged me to be "rough, tough and nasty."

I became scared of the dark while living in Albany. I suppose it was because I was sleeping in a room by myself. At any rate my parents bought me a wire-haired fox terrier, who slept in an old champagne crate right next to my bed. I could reach out my hand and pat her.

She was named Nancy, for one of the characters in a favorite book of mine, *Swallows and
Amazons*. When I went off to boarding school
she was handed over to Harmon Sawyer, the
caretaker for Willow Point. He had grown very
attached to her.

While in Albany I had a lead molding
machine with molds to cast a variety of lead
soldiers. I used a glass of water to cool off any
imperfectly-cast soldier. One day. I dipped a
faulty soldier into the water and then dropped
it back into the melting pot. The molten lead
exploded, splattering lead on the ceiling. Bits
of lead remained stuck to the ceiling and stayed
there for the rest of the time I lived in that
room. I never told anybody about the event,
and I don't think my parents ever knew.

I never put a wet lead soldier into the lead
pot again.

CHAPTER 4

Trip to Europe

I n the spring of 1930, my parents took my brothers, me and Mrs. Sitser, my nurse, to Europe to visit my mother's family. We sailed on the SS Washington from New York City to Hamburg, Germany where we were met by two cars and driven to Aalholm, my grandfather's castle in Denmark. The castle had a moat and a dungeon and was huge. (When my parents were married there in 1918 only 60 people were invited because that was all the guests the castle could accommodate.) The castle had been built as a coastal fortress and had become a royal castle in 1375. The Raben-Levetzau family bought it from King Frederik IV in 1725. I can remember looking down at the dungeon from a trap door in the floor of a room. I remember how big the castle was and how many servants there were.

In the summer of 1932, we went to Europe again, all five of us and my nurse, Mrs. Sitser. We sailed on the SS Europa from New York City to Hamburg and were met there by cars from Aalholm. My brothers and I had been exposed to measles before we left and sure enough the three of us came down with them. Staying at the castle at that time was Count Karl Haugwitz–Reventlow, a former husband of Barbara Hutton. He was not best pleased when he caught measles from the Osborne boys.

When we had recovered my parents took Richard and Devens on a road trip, leaving me behind with my nurse. I was feeling lonely, so Mrs. Sitser tried to cheer me. She reminded me several times that my parents had promised to bring me a present. I became obsessed with the promised present. When they returned and opened the trunk of the car, I grabbed a large brown paper package, convinced it was the promised present. It turned out to be a deflated inner tube. I was outraged, particularly when my father started to laugh at me. I proceeded to kick him several times, which only made him laugh even more. I cannot remember if I was given a present, but I do know I was teased for years afterwards about kicking my father.

During that same visit I was given a present by my grandfather, a set of studs and cufflinks of gold, each surrounding a small ruby. I still have the studs. The cufflinks were stolen by a man who worked for us when my parents were living in Washington.

My grandfather, Count Frederik Christian Raben-Levetzau, was the largest private landowner in Denmark. In those times properties were entailed meaning they were all left to the oldest male heir. My great-grandfather's ancestors had either not married or had had no sons. As a result, he had inherited six country estates and a house in Copenhagen. My grandfather had been a diplomat and had served as Danish foreign minister. He was on good terms with Kaiser Wilhelm II, who honored him with the Order of the Red Eagle. The order was represented by an eight-point star made of diamonds with a German insignia of the order in the center. The Kaiser and the Kaiserin also paid a visit to Aalholm. My mother was offered a post as lady in waiting to the Kaiserin, which she turned down. She felt that life at the German court would be a bore. When Germany invaded Belgium in 1914 my grandfather was furious at what his friend had done. He took his decoration to his jeweler and had the German insignia in the center replaced by a jewel. He then gave the decoration to my mother. It now belongs to my son Christopher, whose middle name is Raben–Levetzau.

We came back from Denmark with two pet jackdaws, who looked like small crows and could be tamed. One of them died quite soon, but the other lived for some years. He was permitted to fly freely, which he did, but he would always come back. He was kept in a cage at night and was let loose during the day. He would swoop in and land on my mother's head or on the table at mealtimes. One of his favorite tricks was to push my mother's silver pin box off her bureau and then look down with obvious pleasure at the pins scattered across the floor. If the table was being laid for a dinner party, he would decline to be caught at all and would push around the silverware. The servants loathed him. He was quite fond of me and would land on my head from time to time. He finally ate a pin and died.

CHAPTER 5

My Danish Relatives

My Danish grandmother was born in Paris of American parents. Her mother, Lillie Greenough, who was born in Cambridge, Mass., had been sent to Paris at any early age for voice training. She had a very fine voice and later sang duets with Jenny Lind, the world-famous opera singer. While Lillie was in Paris in 1862, she met and married Charles Moulton, an American banker who lived in Paris. The winter of 1863 was cold, and Lillie received a pair of skates from her mother and was very anxious to try them out. Lillie had skated since she was eight, growing up in Cambridge. She set out on the little lake of Suresnes near her home and near the home of Emperor Napoléon III at Versailles. The ice was beautiful, and there was a crowd around the pond, but nobody was skating. She skated around the pond but nobody else ventured on to the ice. To encourage the others, she took her baby son from his nurse and skated around the pond with him in her arms. The result was that some of the would-be skaters ventured out onto the ice. When she had returned her baby to the nurse and was watching the skaters Emperor Napoleon III stumbled over to her and said, "Dare I ask such a perfect skater as you to skate with so humble a skater as myself." He took her hand and they set off, he stumbling and she holding him up. At the end of their tour, they stopped in front of the Empress Eugenie. The Emperor urged his wife to skate with Lillie, which she did. Their tour of the lake was a success, and this was how Lillie was introduced to Parisian society. She and the Emperor and Empress remained friends until he died in early 1873. They were invited to a house party at the Versailles palace, Napoleon's principal abode.

The summer of 1934 my parents went off to Europe with Devens and Richard leaving me and my nurse to stay with my Uncle Charles and

Aunt Edith. Mr. and Mrs. Samuel Adams came to dinner one night. She was a former actress and my godmother, and he was a prolific and very successful author. He wrote the story which became the hit movie "It Happened One Night". She, if she became annoyed with him, would refer to him as "you great big god-damned fool." I was coming down the stairs as they arrived and greeted him cheerfully by saying "hullo you great big god-damned fool." I suspect Mrs. Adams and my aunt and uncle were very amused. Mr. Adams was not.

My Uncle Charles was very kind to us when we were growing up and often, when we shook hands with him, we would find ourselves being handed a crisp dollar bill. One time when he did this I rushed off and flushed the bill down the toilet. I have never, never been able to figure out why I did so. However, it is another one of those things my family never let me forget. In the summer of 1935, I was sent to Meenahga Lodge, a summer camp for boys in the Adirondacks. (In the winter the camp became the Adirondack-Florida School.) Johnny Case and Billy Hills, friends from Auburn, went to the camp as well. The camp was on Clear Pond, a peaceful lake in the middle of a wilderness. I enjoyed it thoroughly. When I came back from camp, I rushed into the house to look for Mrs. Sitser. I was devastated when I was told that she had gone. This was particularly true as Devens told me that this was what happened when people grew old and that she would probably die soon.

During the summer of 1936 we all went to Europe again, this time taking with us a Hudson car. We left Quebec on the Empress of Britain and landed in Southampton. On the second day of our travels, we arrived at Salisbury with Richard having a severe pain in his stomach. A doctor was summoned, and Richard was taken to a nursing home (country hospital) where his appendix was removed. He was told to remain in bed for three weeks, so we canceled our plan to go to Scotland and took day trips in England instead. My parents rented a house and found a cook and a maid to look after us.

We visited my Uncle Siegfried and Aunt Pauline, who had a place not far away. Our cousins Peter, Anastasia, Charlotte, and Michael were also there. Visiting them was a friend, Lady Patricia Douglas, the daughter of the Marquis of Queensbury. She and her mother were scheduled to go to Canada, possibly on the Empress of Britain. On the way back to Salisbury my brother Devens grilled my father as to what it meant to be a marquis and if an American could marry the daughter of a marquis. Later my father told my mother that he thought Dev was smitten with Lady Pat. I was in the back seat of the car and overheard the conversation.

My parents decided I needed dressier clothes and took me to a shop called the Fifty Shilling Tailors. I was equipped with a gray flannel jacket and matching gray flannel shorts. Everything was fine until we discovered that the trousers lacked belt loops and required suspenders. My father went back to the store and asked for suspenders. He was given a package which had suspenders written on it. When we opened it, we found a set of sock garters, designed to hold up one's socks. We found that what we wanted were called braces, the British term for suspenders. What we called garters, they called suspenders. We purchased some braces, and my trousers were supported very nicely.

When Richard was able to travel, we took a motor trip through France and Germany.

In Germany we drove on the Reichauto-bahns, which were like the New York State Thruway of today. We had never seen anything like them and were very impressed. My father said the Germans had built them so that they could move troops and supplies quickly. He said that this meant the Germans were planning to go to war. (Three years later he was proved right.) We ended our trip at Cherbourg and boarded the Empress for our trip home. Once on board I found some of the ship's statio-nery and penned the following letter: "Dear Dev, did you know I was on bord? Come to my cabin 417 at 7 PM. Laidy Pat (My spelling left much to be desired in those days.)

I put the letter in an envelope, addressed it to Devens and slipped it under the door of his cabin. He took a bath, slicked down his hair, put on a suit and started urging all of us to go to dinner at six o'clock. He left the dinner table just before seven o'clock and did not return. Apparently, he went to cabin 417, saw a large pair of men's shoes and decided the letter was a fake. I feared that he would take physical revenge, but he did not, taking the lofty view that he had known all along that the letter was a fake. My father was much amused. He kept the letter, pointing out my misspelled words. I later found it in my father's safe deposit box when I was settling his estate. I gave it to Devens who destroyed it.

CHAPTER 6

Going to Boarding School

In the fall of 1937, I was sent to the Adirondack-Florida School. The school had about 40 boys and eight masters. My father, my uncles and my brothers had all gone there. Indeed, my brother Devens was still there during my first year. After that he went to Deerfield Academy.

The school had two campuses, one in the Adirondacks and the other in Coconut Grove, Florida. The fall and spring terms were in the Adirondacks and the winter term in Florida. I took English, Math, Latin, Outdoor Science, and history. As all the classes were exceedingly small, I knew I was going to be called on often. As a result, I was careful to be well prepared. After four years there I went on to Deerfield and found myself ahead of my classmates and the work relatively easy.

In 1941, during my first fall term at Deerfield, the Japanese bombed Pearl Harbor. I can remember hearing Franklin Roosevelt on the radio telling us that December 7th was "a date that would live in infamy."

That February I came down with an extremely high fever and was put to bed and told to stay there. I do not think that I could have gotten out of bed even if I had wanted to. I was not to know then that I would be in bed until the following September. The doctor determined that I had rheumatic fever, and I was taken to an Albany hospital by ambulance. I was impressed that we had a State Police motorcycle escort after we crossed the New York State border. (Kindness of Maj. Warner, I believe.)

I was told that rheumatic fever had caused my heart to grow substantially larger, and that any activity would damage my heart permanently. I took this warning seriously and resigned myself to staying in bed all the time. In the beginning the doctor came every day, listened to my heart, and marked its expansion to the other side of my chest. I did not feel particularly ill, but I also did not want to get out of bed either. I spent about three weeks in the hospital and then was taken by ambulance to the Swan Street house. Two attendants carried me up to the third floor where a hospital bed had been installed in my parents' bedroom. I assume my parents slept in my bedroom which was across the hall. All my needs were tended to by a trained nurse, my mother, and the maid. My days were filled with reading (about a book a day), games (chess, backgammon, Russian bank, gin rummy, piquet, and solitaire), and listening to the radio (in those days there were daily serials). I had a sling shot in the shape of a pistol which enabled me to fire a pellet across the room at a target. I do not recall being petulant, but I fear I must have been from time to time. I can never recall my mother being cross with me although coping with me must have been a challenge.

I also learned to knit and knitted a blue woolen baby's blanket for my cousin Agnes's newly arrived daughter Sara. My cousin Agnes was my Uncle Charles's only daughter. I enjoyed the knitting but have never tried anything else since then. The blanket, as I recall, was handsome. It was made of blue wool yarn My knitting needles were made of wood and were about a foot long. I wondered what had happened to it and asked Sara. She had no memory of it.

When the time came to move to Willow Point, I was taken by ambulance to the railroad station. The ambulance attendants carried me on a stretcher into the station and put me through a window into a sleeping car compartment and thus to bed. The train made a special stop at Port Byron, where I was removed on another stretcher, put in an ambulance, and taken to the Point. I was lodged in a hospital bed in the south bedroom of the guest house. The bed was on wheels and could be rolled outside. My father had a ramp built which was connected to sections of the dock. In this way I could be rolled out onto the lawn when the weather was fair. Being outside was an immense pleasure, even if I was in bed. I had a pair of field glasses and was able to watch the boat traffic on the lake. Also, I had my .32-20 caliber rifle which I used for target practice and to shoot at a woodchuck who appeared from time to time. I never did hit him. When I fired at him, he would leap into the air and then scurry back into the lilac bushes. Then a few days later he would appear again. One would think that he would have looked for a quieter place to live. My nurse would put up the targets on the maple tree that supported the swing. After I had fired a certain number of shots, she would collect the paper target so that I could see the results of my shooting. I will never forget watching her walking across the lawn in her white uniform carrying a fresh target.

Another memory of that summer was Ann Stewart, a girl slightly older than I. She would paddle up the lake in her canoe to play gin rummy with me. The Stewarts lived on a point about half a mile to the south of us on the same side of the lake. She paddled because gasoline was in short supply and rationed. I enjoyed our games and her company very much. It became a friendship which has continued to this day.

I was taught chess by my mother. While I was sick several adults kindly came to the Point to play against me. Later, at school I won the chess championship my junior year but lost in the finals my senior year. Also, I played on the chess team against Andover, losing my match.

My great-grandmother, Eliza Wright Osborne, who had been a great reader, had had twenty years of *The Strand Magazine* bound. They included the original publication of many of the Sherlock Holmes stories. They were a change from my other reading fare.

That summer my father was working in Albany and would come home only on weekends. Richard was in his senior year at Harvard and preparing to go into the Navy and Devens was at the University of Arizona. In September, while I was finally able to get out of bed, my activities were still severely limited, and life continued to be confining. In November, my mother and I took the train to Tucson, where my brother Devens was attending the university. We stayed at the Tanque Verde Ranch, which was a combination dude and cattle ranch, owned and run by Jim Converse and his second wife, Kay. After my mother had me settled in, she left me there and went back East. I still had to be careful not to exert myself too much, but I was able to ride most days. Kay entertained me at the backgammon board, but happily not for money as she was a steady winner. When the Christmas season rolled around Barbie Converse, Jim's daughter, came back from boarding school for the holidays. The Converses gave a Christmas party for the guests and invited my brother Devens to come, which he did. He and Barbie fell very much in love at that party. (They continued to see each other after the party and were married in November of 1944.)

After Christmas, the doctor said my health was good enough to go back to school and I was sent to the Southern Arizona School for Boys. The school was enthusiastic about horses, and one was bought for me. He was big and amiable and was named Tex. I was devoted to him. I was perfectly happy at the school and was prepared to continue my education there the following fall. My father had different ideas. Over my protestations he insisted that I go back to Deerfield. As things turned out, he was quite right, although I did not think so at the time. I suspect he felt my chances of getting into Harvard would be better if I went back to Deerfield.

In June of 1943 Richard finished his Naval training and received his commission as an ensign. He and Mary Morse were married at the River Club in New York City shortly afterward. Devens was best man, and I was an usher. Everything had changed with the war. My father had gone to work for the US Office of Strategic Services (later the Central Intelligence Agency) in Washington, Richard was in the Navy and Devens was still at the University of Arizona.

CHAPTER 7

Summer at Willow Point During the War

I spent the summer of 1943 at the Point with my mother. I tended the victory garden and looked after a sow pig and four piglets who were quartered in the garage/stable. (Because of food shortages during the war, people who otherwise would not have done so, turned lawns and flower beds into what were known as victory gardens.) We raised peas, spinach, corn, potatoes, and turnips in ours. We ate some, sold some to the railroad crews and the Osborne Hotel and gave some away. The pigs were all taken to the butcher in Moravia at the end of the summer. We ate some of the meat and the rest was sold. I never grew attached to those pigs and was perfectly happy to see them go off at the end of the summer.

I had owned a rifle since I was twelve and used it that summer, hunting woodchucks or for target practice. I also owned a 20-gauge shotgun. I used that to break clay pigeons and later for shooting skunks and racoons. I was never a very good shot. I did shoot one woodchuck which I skinned. My mother cooked a portion of it which turned out, as I recall, to be rather sweet tasting. Because of gasoline shortages during the war, we went to town infrequently. My mother would order the groceries by telephone and have them delivered to the Lehigh Valley Railroad station in Auburn. There they were loaded into a freight car to be taken to the Point. At the Point the train would stop, the conductor would break the seal on the freight car door, open it and hand my mother her order. From time to time, we would sell the train crew the fresh vegetables we were raising in our victory garden. That fall I went back to Deerfield for my junior year.

During the summer of 1944 I worked on Fred Wiant's dairy farm and helped in our garden. The Wiant farm was just outside the hamlet of Scipio. He had about thirty cows which had to be milked twice a day. I did not help with the actual milking but did help cleaning the milking machinery and shoveling out the barn. I drove Fred's team of horses to cultivate the corn and to cut and harvest the hay. We stored the hay in the loft of the barn. I was paid $3 a day.

Occasionally Fred and I helped his father who had a farm not too far away. Fred's father told me that his grandfather would tell him about going down to the Point to watch Civil War volunteers march along the plank road going off to war. Every now and then when I walk down that road, I wonder how many of those volunteers came home.

That fall I went back to Deerfield for my senior year. Because of a shortage of help the area farmers did not have the workforce to harvest their potato crop. Time was short as the potatoes were scheduled to be shipped overseas shortly. The farmers asked for assistance and the whole school took the day off and picked up the whole potato crop. We were gratified that we had been able to help the war effort.

During my senior year I turned eighteen in October and registered for the draft. The

Cayuga County draft board allowed me to finish the school year before I had to go, which pleased me enormously. Frank Boyden, the headmaster, had all our senior class apply for college admission whether we were going into the armed forces or not. I applied to Harvard and was accepted. My father had told me I could go to college anywhere I wished, but that he would pay my way to Harvard. Little did he or I know that most of my college tuition would be paid by the GI Bill. I have always been glad that I applied when I did.

In November 1944 Franklin Roosevelt won his fourth term as president. After the election he appointed my father as ambassador to the Norwegian government in exile and my parents sailed for London on the Queen Mary, which was being used as a troop ship. At that time London was being attacked by the Germans with rockets known as buzz bombs. Their engines made a noise until their motors cut off and the bombs would come down on their targets. My father told of hearing the buzz bombs coming, while my mother was asleep. She would wake up the next morning and say cheerfully "Well, there were no bangs last night." My father, who had been up all night listening to the bombs, always said he was never able to think of a sufficiently cutting rejoinder.

That fall Devens and Barbie were married at St. James Church in Manhattan with a reception at the River Club afterwards. I was best man. As my parents were in London, I spent that Christmas vacation at 99 with Dev and Barbie. Dev was working at Alco Products in Auburn. It was our family custom to hang stockings in front of the fireplace on Christmas Eve in the hope that they would be filled. Dev, Barbie, and I decided to skip the custom and we went off to the midnight service at St. Peter's Church. Imagine our astonishment when we returned from church to find our stockings filled with presents and hanging in front of the fireplace. It was a complete and total surprise at a time when we were missing our parents. The stockings were put up and filled by my Uncle Charles, Aunt Edith, and Uncle David. It was a kindness which I have never forgotten. David and Charles were my father's older brothers.

That spring vacation I spent with Charlie Bassett, a Deerfield classmate, at his family's home in Kennebunk, Maine. Two highlights of that visit were a town hall meeting and a "sugaring off" party. The first was the Kennebunkport annual town meeting. Most of the residents of the township attended and settled the affairs of the township for the coming year by a vote of all residents present. It was an example of democracy in its purest form. The town employee who ran the snowplow, made an impassioned plea for a raise. After considerable discussion he was voted a ten cent an hour raise. There was also a discussion as to which roads, if any, should be improved and when. I still wonder from time to time if the annual meeting was deliberately held before the summer visitors arrived in Kennebunkport.

The other event was a "sugaring off" party at a local farm. The process involved a large, black wood stove with a brisk fire and a large collection of pots jammed on the stove's surface. The pots had been filled with maple tree sap, which was boiling away and giving off the most delectable smell. The sap was boiled down until it became maple syrup or, if boiled more, maple sugar. We were served pancakes with maple syrup on them. They were delicious. To collect the sap an incision was made in a maple tree and a bucket attached to the tree. As the sap started to rise in the spring it would run into the bucket. When the buckets were full, they were collected and the sugaring off process begun.

CHAPTER 8

In the Army

That May Germany surrendered, but we were still at war with Japan. In June I graduated from Deerfield with Uncle Charles and Aunt Edith in attendance, replacing my parents who were in Oslo with the Norwegian government. Since I was going off to the army Aunt Edith had insisted that I should be confirmed as an Episcopalian. The Rev. Malcolm E. Peabody, bishop of the Central New York Episcopal diocese, presided. He was a classmate and friend of my Uncle Charles, and I had met him from time to time when he dined with my aunt and uncle. My parents, who never went to church unless it was somebody's wedding or funeral, had been quite uninterested in my religious upbringing. Most of my religious exposure had come at boarding schools where there had been a service every day except Sunday, when there were two services. I have always been glad my aunt insisted.

Three weeks after my Deerfield graduation I was on a bus to Syracuse and inducted into the US Army. The bus took us to the Syracuse armory, where we were given physical exams, found fit, given serial numbers, and sworn into the army. I remember the song "Don't Fence Me In" was being played on the loudspeaker.

We were transported to Fort Dix, New Jersey, where the induction process continued. The army fitted us out with uniforms and gave us boxes in which we could send our civilian clothes home. They also apparently were deciding what to do with us. After a few days I was put on a special train filled with draftees. We were not told where we were going. The train trip, in coaches with no air conditioning, took two days. The windows were all open because of the heat, which caused the smoke from the engine to blow into the cars. It was a miserable trip. Our journey ended at Camp Blanding, an infantry basic training center in the middle of Florida. Here we were to get seventeen weeks of basic infantry training. We were told that the army had trained a million infantrymen at the camp. When our training was over, we were to be sent as replacements in various infantry units. I was assigned to a barracks with 20 other men. Most of my barrack mates were about my age, some from upstate New York and others from the western part of North Carolina. Some had never left home before. I found that, with seven years of boarding school behind me, I had less trouble than most of them in adjusting to army life. We were given M-1 .30 caliber rifles, which were standard issue for the army at that time. Since I had owned a rifle since the age of twelve, this was nothing new to me. However, the M-1 did work differently than my .32-20 Winchester lever action rifle. Bazookas, flame throwers, machine guns, and gas masks were new to me and interesting. There was a mock Japanese village which we practiced capturing, and I recall throwing live grenades through the windows as part of the exercise. At that time the army was strictly segregated, with Blacks restricted to construction units. I remember one fellow soldier saying the reason for this was "that the N***** lacked the stomach to fight." I wish I had known then about the 369th Infantry Regiment which fought in World War I and was known as the Harlem Hell Fighters. I could have told him it was the most decorated unit in the US army in that war.

In early August, our lieutenant told us about a new bomb which had been dropped on Japan and shortly afterwards the Japanese surrendered. We were all relieved that we would not have to invade the main island of Japan. The fierce fighting during the landings on Okinawa had given everyone a picture of how tough a battle it would have been. It was hot in August when we went on a six mile march, complete with rifle, helmet, and full pack. When we had a break the sergeant said "smoke them if you've got them". Everybody was dripping with sweat and could not light damp cigarettes with damp matches. I looked at them struggling and thought if you have to do all that to smoke, it isn't worth it. As a result, I have never smoked.

With the coming of peace, the training was more relaxed, although we did spend two weeks living in tents on bivouac. The weather had turned colder, and I was sleeping on the ground in my tent. My blanket was too short for me, so I took to putting my feet in my duffle bag to keep them warm. Coral snakes, which are deadly poisonous, frequented that part of Florida and we had to be on the alert for them. Rattlesnakes were also a problem. The army had imported pigs to attack the snakes. Unfortunately, the pigs were also inclined to raid our food supplies and had to be guarded against.

When basic training ended, I was given orders to report to the Coastal Artillery School at Fort Monroe, Virginia. The fort had been built after the War of 1812 to guard Chesapeake Bay and had been a military base ever since. I was assigned, as part of the permanent staff, to a barrack that must have held about eighty men. It was then that I had a big stroke of good luck. In the bunk next to me was a man named Thomas Treveal, whose father was my Uncle Charles's chauffeur. He was the company clerk and one day he told me that a course in radar maintenance and operation was opening at the school, that it was a great chance, and that I should apply. I did and was accepted. As a result, I spent the next five months going to school learning about electronics and radar and not standing guard duty, cleaning cannons, or doing KP. It was very much like being back in school, and I enjoyed it thoroughly. Because I was so tall, the army had never been able to provide me with a properly fitting overcoat. As a result, I was told to stay in our barracks when our unit was standing inspection. I was able to take weekend leave and to go up to Washington to visit my cousin Agnes and her husband Gussie. It was a wonderful break from the military. To get to Washington I would take a bus from the base to Newport News and then another bus to Washington.

To go back, Gussie would drive me to the last stoplight in Alexandria and I would check the cars until I found one with Richmond on the license plate. I would rap on the window and ask if they would take me to Richmond. I was in uniform and usually they would. Once in Richmond I would take the streetcar to the last stoplight on the road to Newport News and start rapping on windows. The system worked well almost all the time. But once my lift to Newport News stopped in the middle of nowhere because they were turning down a side road. I stepped out into the dark with not a light in sight and started sticking out my thumb. I had no idea what I was going to do if I did not get a ride. There were few cars, and they did not stop. Finally, a car stopped, and I opened the back door. All I could see were some white teeth in black faces. I had never met, let alone known, any African Americans, and this was quite a shock. I hesitated for about one second and then climbed in and gratefully accepted a ride to the bus station. I am still grateful for that ride.

Another time, the car ahead of us turned over on a curve and rolled over and continued to roll over as it went down a hill. We stopped to investigate. As I started down the hill to investigate a woman appeared with blood streaming down her face. She collapsed into my arms, and I carried her up to the road and into a nearby house. An ambulance arrived shortly afterwards, and she was carried away. My ride was leaving so I went with them and never found out what happened to the woman.

After the radar course ended, I returned to my unit. The army had decided to transfer the Coast Artillery School to the West Coast and our unit was put on an army troop transport bound for San Francisco and the Pacific. The trip was the most unpleasant ocean voyage I have ever taken. The double rows of bunks were three high, side by side and head to toe; the showers had salt water; and the two meals a day were mostly uneatable. Added to that the voyage to Panama was very rough and I was seasick. When we arrived in Panama the air conditioning broke down and we were transferred to a barracks in the Canal Zone until the ship was repaired. It took a week to repair the ship. When that was completed the trip to San Francisco was resumed, leaving from the other end of the canal. I never saw the canal. The Coast Artillery School was stationed at Fort Funston, a small installation on the outskirts of San Francisco next to a golf course. If nothing was happening, we would go over the back fence to the golf course and hire ourselves out as caddies. As I recall I received $20 for carrying two golf bags for eighteen holes. One day our unit received a call from a coast artillery station across San Francisco Bay that their radar unit was not operating correctly. I was sent over to see if I could fix it. I was taken to a site on a rocky hill on the north side of the bay. At first glance, I did not see anything but a view of the Pacific. Then I noticed a hatch cover. I lifted it up and saw there was a ladder down the side of the shaft. I climbed down, found a light switch, and followed a passage which led to a radar set. I sat down, turned the set on and started trying to find out what the problem was.

As I was working, I heard a voice behind me saying "What the hell are you doing and how did you get in here?" I turned to see a lieutenant and another man standing in the doorway. I explained that I had been sent to fix the radar set and that the hatch cover had been open. The lieutenant turned pale at the news that the hatch cover had been open but let me continue working on the set. When I had it running, I found that it was monitoring the entrance to San Francisco Bay. I still wonder at the lack of security and wonder if somebody was severely reprimanded because that hatch cover was left unlocked.

One day a message arrived that General Fredericks, the commander of the Coast Artillery School, wanted to see me. To say that my sergeant had a fit was putting things mildly. He gave me a careful inspection to make sure that I was properly attired in my dress uniform before I was sent off. It turned out that the general had been my father's military attaché in Oslo. My mother had made my father call him up. She wanted to make sure that I was all right. I assured the general that I was fine, and we agreed that mothers tended to worry overly much. With that I was dismissed. From time to time our unit was sent to a firing station south of San Francisco and near Carmel and Pebble Beach. When on station we practiced shooting the cannons at targets being towed in the ocean. The shell splashes would show up on the radar screen and we could tell the gunners how close to the target they were.

At that time Richard and Mary were in the East while he was going to the Cornell Hotel School. However, Mary's parents were living in Pebble Beach, and I was given a weekend pass to go down to visit them. Mary's parents were busy, so Richard and Mary's friends kindly took me under their collective wing. One night Stuyvie Fish, Richard's college roommate, his date, and another couple invited me to go with them to a nightclub. I discovered that Stuyvie had as his date, Ann Southern, a popular movie actress of that era. She caused a stir when we came into the nightclub. While the others chatted away, I stayed still and functioned as the audience. Looking around, I spotted the lieutenant of my unit across the room. I looked away quickly, hoping he had not seen me, and trying to think what I would say and do if he were to come over to our table. He did not come over, to my great relief. The following Monday he came up to me and asked, "Wasn't that Ann Southern at the table with you on Saturday night?" I had decided that if I were asked, the best response was to be totally blasé. I said "Yes, it was" and did not elaborate further and he did not pursue the subject.

In October I happened to read a news item saying that soldiers who had been in the army for a year and had been accepted in college could be immediately discharged. I called up my father to say that I thought I qualified, and could he find out if I did qualify. Shortly afterward we went down to the firing point. While at the firing point our unit communicated with Fort Funston by a shortwave radio located in the unit's orderly room. A few days later I was called to the orderly room and told a telegram had come for me. The telegram, from my father, was read to me over the radio as follows "Have called Gen Fredericks concerning your discharge. Stop. Expect to see you at Harvard within the week. Stop. Love, Daddy."

As I had expected to be in the army at least another eight months or more, I was naturally elated. However, I was also very embarrassed. Our unit was filled with men who had been in the army longer than I had been and were just as anxious to be discharged. I shuddered to think how angry they must feel. Anyhow the unit's captain sent me back to San Francisco in his jeep and I was on my way to Harvard.

CHAPTER 9

Harvard

I took planes from San Francisco to Boston via Los Angeles, Texas and Chicago and registered at Harvard. I was assigned a room in Mower Hall with two roommates, Eliot Putnam and Stuart Edmonds. I knew Eliot since we had been at Deerfield together. Stuart was new to me but seemed pleasant. They had both been in the service. I decided to take courses in English, math, French and history. One of my first steps was to go to Newell boathouse to sign up for freshman crew. I had never rowed in an eight-oared shell before, but my father and Richard had, and I decided to give it a try. The coach, Harvey Love, took one look at me and said, "if I can't make an oarsman out of you, I am going to quit." He nearly had to.

After a week I went down to Camp Dix, New Jersey, to get my discharge. I was amused that in the evenings, when my barracks mates went off to the Post Exchange bar to celebrate, I stayed put as I was trying to catch up on my history course.

It took about a week to go through all the army's physical examinations and paperwork. Finally, it was done, and I had gone from an army private to a Harvard freshman. It was a relief. Looking back, my time in the army was very lonely. My background was so different from my fellow soldiers that it was difficult for me to connect with them. I never made any close friends that I kept up with after I was discharged. I never told anybody that I had gone to a private school, that my father was an ambassador, that my mother had been a countess or that I was going to Harvard. I thought doing so would be a mistake. I remember being told of the GI Bill by my sergeant who said that it would pay my way to college. When I said I would go to college anyway he did not believe me.

While I was in basic training, I saw a poster by the cartoonist Al Capp pinned to the bulletin board. It portrayed a Daisy Mae type and urged GIs to buy war bonds. I was so taken by the poster that I removed it. It still hangs in my office.

When I got back to Cambridge from Camp Dix my mother came from Auburn to see me. She brought with her a suitcase filled with my civilian clothes. She was staying at the Chilton Club, a club for society ladies on Beacon Street in Boston, and we were to lunch there. As a special favor, I was permitted to go up to the second floor to exchange my uniform for a sports jacket, gray flannels, and a cheerful tie. It was a delight finally to be quit of the army. Up to that point, I had been wearing my uniform to classes.

When I first started my classes I had considerable academic problems and my grades were not good. This was a jolt, as I had never had any academic problems when I was in boarding school. However, once I had settled down, I managed a large collection of "C's" and the occasional "B". In retrospect I did not work as hard as I should have and failed to take advantage of the scholastic richness that Harvard had to offer. My mind was more preoccupied with crew and with my social life. After I received my BA degree I was accepted in graduate school, the first year in the Graduate School of Public Administration and the second year at the Harvard Business School. I did better academically in graduate school than I did in college.

My father, who had been appointed ambassador to Norway by Franklin Roosevelt, had resigned when the President died, as was the custom. No action had been taken on his resignation until May of 1946, when he asked that it be accepted, and he and my mother came home. Not long after, he accepted an appointment as president of the American-Scandinavian Foundation. The foundation had offices in New York City and my parents spent their time between the City and Auburn. They lived in an apartment in the foundation's building on East 73rd St. I could stay there when I was in New York.

That spring I rowed on the second freshman boat for most of the spring and in the combination crew for the Yale races on the Thames at New London, Conn. The combination crew was made up of substitutes for the freshman and junior varsity crews. We trained for two weeks at Red Top; a training camp built especially for the Yale race.

Sadly, our boat lost—the first Harvard crew to lose to Yale since before the war.

CHAPTER 10
Going to Norway

I had been planning to spend the summer between my freshman and sophomore years at Willow Point, having missed two summers there because of the army. But my father had different plans. He had established an American summer school at the University of Oslo and was very anxious that I attend. So, I attended.

We sailed on a converted C-4 transport, like the one I had sailed on going to San Francisco, but far more comfortable. While it did not compare with the ocean liners that I had sailed on in the 1930s, it was comfortable enough and it was getting us to Europe. Almost all the passengers were students going abroad for the summer, which made for a very cheery trip.

We sailed from New York, first to Cherbourg and then to Oslo. The Norwegians were most welcoming then and all through our stay. We lived at the university and ate in its dining hall. The food was a Norwegian version of what I had been eating at Harvard. From time to time, however, we were given whale meat. I never acquired a taste for whale meat. I think that the thing that bothered the Americans the most was the fact that the beer was not cold. Some of the time it was not even barely chilled.

I was invited to a picnic by Oivind Lorent-zian, a friend of my father. Herr Lorentzian picked me up at the university and we drove for about an hour. Then he announced that we had arrived at the edge of his property. Then we drove for another hour until we reached his house. (I wondered how he managed to own so much land in a country which was essentially socialist.) Among those at the picnic were Dag Hammarskjold, secretary general of the United Nations, and Crown Prince Olaf of Norway. The Secretary General and the Crown Prince were having an animated conversation but, since it was in Norwegian, I was not able to understand it.

The Norwegians went in for shaking hands on all occasions. Our group was taken to one party where we all lined up and one by one shook hands with the two Norwegian princesses Ragnhild and Astrid.

The Norsk Studenten Rodeklub (Norwegian Student Rowing Club) very kindly let the American students use their rowing facilities and I had a very pleasant time rowing around Oslo harbor in a single shell. The club also had something called en kone bot (a wife boat), which had outriggers and a sliding seat and a seat for the kone (wife) in the stern. I persuaded Polly Kinnear, the girl I admired at that moment, to go for a ride. She loved it, particularly as we happened to see some of our fellow students on our trip around the harbor. When our course ended, I went down to Copenhagen to visit my Uncle Emil and Aunt Suzanne Lassen and their daughter, my cousin Bente. From there I took a train through Germany. That trip left a lasting impression on me. The train ran through town after town where there was nothing but the pushed down steel skeletons of buildings with piles of bricks underneath them. The streets had been cleared by throwing bricks into mounds on either side of the street. This desolation was all the result of Allied bombing and gave me a firsthand look at the ravages of war.

After a few days exploring Paris Polly Kinnear and I and another couple went on a bicycle trip to Reins. We visited the cathedral and slept in a haystack one night and in a vineyard another night. Then I went on to Cherbourg and back to the States. I arrived just in time to register for my sophomore year. Eliot, Stuart, and I had not been given a place in one of the Harvard houses but had rooms in Apley Court, a Harvard dormitory near the Harvard Yard. We ate, as we had in our first year, at the Harvard Union.

The fall of sophomore year was the time when Harvard's final clubs selected members. Some of the clubs had started out as branches of national fraternities, but had broken away, not caring for visitors from the fraternities of other colleges. My father, uncles and brother had all been members of the Delphic Club. I was not asked to join, for reasons which I never discovered. I was upset but could do nothing about it. I was asked to join the Iroquois Club but turned down the invitation. One could belong to only one final club, and I decided to wait to see if the Delphic Club changed its mind. Eliot had joined the Spee Club and the next fall I was invited to join there and accepted. My cousin, Jim Storrow, was also a member. I learned later that the Delphic Club was planning to elect me but that the Spee had acted first. The final club members, who made up about ten percent of the class, came almost entirely from the elite Eastern boarding schools. There were several Deerfield graduates in the Spee, and I enjoyed my time there very much. While Jack and Bobby Kennedy were both members of the club, they had graduated before I joined. and I never met them at the club. The only time I did meet Bobby was at a political rally at the Polish Home camp outside Auburn. I went up to him and said that we were probably the only two Democrats who belonged to the Spee Club. He took one look at me and hurried off.

I tried out for the varsity crew but was not successful. I was on the squad in the third boat for the whole season, but never made the second boat. As a result, I never raced against other colleges during the regular season.

When summer vacation came, I went back

to Auburn and went to work for *The Citizen-Advertiser* part-time. I went to typing school in the mornings and to the paper in the afternoons, typing up social notes, weddings, and obituaries. That summer was the 100th Anniversary of the issuance of the Women's Rights Declaration of Sentiment, which my great-great-grandmother, Martha Coffin Wright, had helped to write. My Uncle Charles took me away from the newsroom to accompany him to the ceremony. Nobody in the family had ever talked much about suffragettes and I can remember being bored with the whole proceeding. Only later did I realize the significance of the declaration.

I recall writing a social note reporting that Mr. and Mrs. Maurice I Schwartz had done something, I cannot recall exactly what it was. The next day there was a call from Mr. Schwartz saying that Mrs. Schwartz had died some years before. I had simply assumed incorrectly that Mr. Schwartz was married. I learned from that error that you do not assume things in the newspaper business. By the end of the summer, I had learned to type reasonably well and was writing brief stories, which the city editor would critique. It was a start, albeit a slow one, into learning the news-paper business.

That fall Eliot, Stuart, and I moved to A Entry in Eliot House, where upperclassmen were housed. I joined the Spee Club and more of my college life centered around the club. I frequently lunched there and found backgammon opponents. We played for beers, which cost twenty-five cents in those days. I was more than able to hold my own and enjoyed myself thoroughly.

That year I was dropped from the varsity squad midway through the spring term and shifted to rowing on the Eliot House crew. At the end of the season, we rowed against the other house crews and were able to beat them all. When I was not rowing in the Eliot eight oared shell, I learned to row in a single shell. At the end of the spring term, I was invited to join Sam Peabody and John Bullitt in their rooms in O Entry. Their third roommate, Tom Aspinwall, had married during the summer and was living with his wife in an apartment in Cambridge.

CHAPTER 11

Another Trip to Europe

Between junior and senior years, I went to Europe again, this time by airplane. I went first to Edenborough where I stayed with the Rev. and Mrs. John Bailee. He had been a visiting professor at the Auburn Theological Seminary and was a friend of my parents. As I recall I did a considerable amount of sightseeing. Sadly, I cannot remember precisely what I saw. From there I went to visit the Gordonstoun School, which was run by Kurt Hahn, a German liberal who had fled to England after being arrested by the Nazis in 1933. Once in England he had started Gordonstoun. He had been a friend of my father when my father was at the U.S. Embassy in Berlin during World War One. Among the notable graduates of the school was Philip, Duke of Edenborough. Gordonstoun, unlike other English public (private in the US) schools, was based on democratic principles with an emphasis on public service.

Mr. Hahn arranged that I should go on a walking trip in the Cairngorm Mountains with Lord Malcolm Douglas-Hamilton, who was a governor of the school; Dr. Stuart MacIntosh, head of the school; and Tidi Lund, a silent but stunning Danish girl. We spent the night at an inn in Aviemore prior to setting out to climb the second highest mountain in the British Isles. I will never forget the moment when Tidi appeared at the top of the stairs at the inn. She was a vision with long very blonde hair, a smiling face, and a beautiful figure. As she came down the stairs the whole lobby went quiet and just gazed at her. I do not think the Highlanders had ever seen anyone quite like her before.

The next day we set out to climb Ben MacDui, the second-highest mountain in Scotland. At the top we were provided with a wonderful view. We also went for a very cold swim in Loch Bouie, the highest body of water in the British Isles. We slept that night part way down the mountain, very cold in inadequate sleeping bags. We walked out the next day and I said goodbye to the others and took the night train to London. While staying in London I saw my cousin Charlotte Raben-Levetzau and other connections and attended a session of the House of Commons. I also did other sightseeing.

I was invited to dinner by the Wendells, British cousins of my Aunt Edith. When they found that I played tennis they invited me to play at the Wimbledon All English Tennis Club, as they were club members. We played the next day on one of the side courts. The courts were grass and I, being accustomed to clay courts, did not play very well. However, it was still exciting to be there.

A few days later Sam Peabody arrived from the US and the next day we set off to visit his sister, Marietta Tree, and her husband Ronnie. The Trees had a splendid 4,000-acre estate named Dytchley outside Oxford. The house had been built for the Earl of Litchfield and was one of the show places of England. Ronnie Tree had been a member of Parliament during the war and Winston Churchill had stayed at Dytchley on weekends for fear that the Germans would try to bomb Chartwell, the Churchills' home. Ronnie's mother had been an American, a daughter of Marshall Field. The house was enormous by my standards. It had two wings, one of which included a private chapel. I was amused to find a framed announcement in a side hall stating a by-election result. It reported that the Conservative, Ronald Tree, had defeated his Labour opponent. Ronnie's occupation was listed as "Gentleman."

The house was well supplied with servants including Collins, the butler, and several footmen. One of these carefully laid out my dinner clothes each evening and put tooth-paste on my toothbrush.

Ronnie was a warden of the local church which held a fête on the grounds while we were there. The event was straight out of P.G. Wodehouse with an egg-in-spoon race, a three-legged race, ice cream, darts, and games of chance. Sam and I assisted as best we could, including judging the finish of the races.

We went back to London in time to attend a fancy-dress ball at the American Embassy. Everyone was supposed to come as the title of a book, song, play or movie. After a considerable debate I went as "Crime" and Sam as "Punishment." The Duke and Duchess of Edinburgh were there as the "Butler and the Upstairs Maid." Princess Margaret and Charmin Douglas were part of a chorus line of Can-Can girls. Ambassador Douglas came as a cowboy with a patch over the eye he had hurt while salmon fishing. I found that the Douglas's had known my parents as they very kindly asked after them. We went back to the hotel slightly after four am.

We had decided to visit Denmark, and after several telephone calls was able to reach my Aunt Suzanne and make arrangements. We set out from London by train and boat to Erlejborg in Denmark and from there to Copenhagen by train. We were met by my cousin Bente and taken to the Lassen apartment in Nyhaven. Nyhaven had a canal down the middle of the street, which provided moorings for smaller boats. It was lined with bars. My aunt and cousin were off to the States the next day, so they arranged for us to stay with another cousin, Andreas Holm. We were well looked after by my relatives during our stay and had a splendid time. A friend of my brother Richard arranged for us to be extras in a movie which was being filmed at Copenhagen airport. The filming started at 11:30 PM and ended, after five retakes, at 4 AM. I was filmed going through currency control behind the hero and my line was to say in English, that I had no dollars to declare. The pay was forty kroner ($10) each. Sadly, I have never seen the movie.

The boat trip to England was smooth. We spent a night in London before going down to Dytchley for a farewell dance. The Trees were selling the house and leaving England because Ronnie was having to pay income taxes in both the US and England.

The house was decorated with masses of flowers and looked beautiful. The dance was a gala affair with a band, champagne, and fireworks. The Duke and Duchess of Edinburgh were there, and I foolishly tried to cut in on the Princess Elizabeth. I was completely ignored. I decided that one did not cut in on a future queen without a previous introduction. I was better behaved than another American, who came up to the duke and said "You must be Albert. I want you to introduce me to Victoria." The duke was not amused.

The next day we went back to London and caught a plane to Paris to meet Harry Guild and

Jim Rossiter, Harvard classmates, with whom we were going to travel in France and Italy. After a few days of seeing the sights in Paris the next step was to rent a car, which we did. It was a six-cylinder Renault sedan, slightly larger than a Volkswagen Beetle. The four of us could barely squeeze into it. We armed ourselves with a Michelin guidebook and set out for Reins. We went to Rouen, Beauvais, and then to the Normandy beaches. Standing on the cliff over the beach I looked down and was very glad I had missed D-Day. We continued south to Biarritz where Sheila Guild, Harry's sister, was visiting the Dubonnet family. Ann Dubonnet had been at school with Sheila in Boston during the war. We had hoped to stay with the Dubonnets but were shuffled off to a hotel instead. We were annoyed at the time but in retrospect, I really cannot blame the Dubonnets for not wanting to cope with four thirsty undergraduates.

Our entertainment while we were there was tennis and swimming. The swimming was done with great caution because there was a dangerous undertow when the tide was going out. In connection with this we were told a story about the German occupation. The

French did not warn the Germans about the undertow. After a number of their soldiers were drowned the Germans finally took to posting sentries on the beach to keep their troops from going into the water.

CHAPTER 12

Casino Visits

I visited the casino twice while I was in Biarritz. During my first visit, I lost $30. On my second visit, I won $15. While in Monte Carlo I won $50 and in Venice, I won $10. My method was to bet on the red or black (a nearly even money bet). I would watch the wheel without betting. If black came up three times I would bet on red and double my bet if I lost. I would continue doubling if I lost until I won, which would leave me ahead by my original wager. I used the same approach later when I was in Reno. I never won much but I did come out ahead. One time the wheel came up black nine times when I had bet on red. I nearly had a fit. On the tenth time, the wheel came up red, and I was ahead by my original bet. I was vastly relieved.

Some years later, when I went to the new casino in Murray Bay, I had a change of heart. I was about to start betting when I looked at the table with its four attendants. Then I looked at the glitter and all the gaudy surroundings and thought "all of this must be paid for before I get any of my money back". I realized that the odds were against me and that I was making a less-than-even money bet. I left the casino and have never gambled at a casino since. I happily play poker, bridge, or backgammon for money with my friends. I have kept careful track of the results for thirty years and invested my winnings in the stock market, another form of gambling. At the moment I am gratefully $144,000 ahead.

After leaving Biarritz we went to Monte Carlo and then on to Rome. Rome was interesting but uneventful except for my trying to exchange money on the black market. The official rate was 400 liras to the dollar while the black-market rate was 600 liras to the dollar. I was about to make an exchange when a police officer appeared and dragged me off to the police station. I was freed after I was made to exchange dollars for lira at the official rate. I still wonder if it was a scam. Did the police officer take my dollars and exchange them himself for lira at the black-market rate? I will never know.

After seeing all the tourist sites, we set off for Venice. On the way I had hoped to stop at the Argenta Gap cemetery where my cousin, Anders Lassen VC MC, a major of the SAS, is buried. However, we were not able to do so. Anders had been killed in April 1945, after a spectacular war career. He was the only person awarded the Victoria Cross, Britain's highest honor, who was not a citizen of the British Commonwealth. He is portrayed in a recent motion picture entitled *The Ministry of Ungentlemanly Warfare*, which tells of one of his first exploits,

I spent two nights in Venice and then left the others and took a train to Milan and another train to Paris. From Paris I flew to London. From there I flew with several stops, to Montreal. From Montreal I took a train to Utica, where I was met by my parents, who drove me to Willow Point. I was in Europe for 80 days.

CHAPTER 13

Back in the States

The next day my parents had a welcome-home fancy dress party for me. The guests were to come as something I had seen or might have seen during my trip. It was a splendid party and a wonderful way to end my trip. Sue Riford, who was in the later stages of a pregnancy, came in a flowing white dress, as a "London fog." My brother Devens came as a British bookie. My father came as a diplomat, complete with all his decorations.

Back at Harvard I decided I would skip fall rowing and play football instead. I joined the Eliot House tackle football squad, which played teams from the other Harvard houses. We had a good team and were undefeated. As a result, we played the Yale intramural champions in New Haven the weekend of the Harvard-Yale game. In the final quarter we were on the Yale 12 yard line and the quarterback called for an end run around the right end. I was playing right tackle and was supposed to pull out of the line and lead the charge. Being exceedingly slow of foot the back I was supposed to protect was ahead of me. However, there was a linebacker in sight, so I knocked him down and the back went on to score. We won 6-0 for an undefeated season.

My cousin Bente was in New York visiting my parents and my father sent her up to watch the game. She was and remains exceedingly attractive. At the cocktail party after the game, I thought that my teammates would flock around Bente. To my surprise they did not. However, John Finley, the Master of Eliot House, was intrigued by her and spent the rest of the party talking to her.

During my senior year I went to a very fashionable dance at Tuxedo Park, the Tuxedo Autumn Ball. While some of my Harvard friends were there, I knew none of the girls. I spotted one very pretty dark-haired girl sitting on the top step of the stairs, smiling and laughing. She looked very attractive. I asked her name from a friend and was told it. I never did meet her, but I certainly saw plenty of pictures of her later on. Her name then was Jackie Bouvier. Later it was Jackie Kennedy.

With the football season over I went back to crew. and was able to make the second varsity. In June when Harvard rowed Yale on the Thames in New London, we beat the Yale JVs by more than a length as part of Harvard's sweep of the river. After the race I weighed 195 pounds. Ever since I have tried to remain under that weight and have mostly succeeded. I currently weigh 175.

That spring my cousins, Tom and Nella Storrow, invited me to dinner before a Boston dance. I sat next to a girl named May Sedgwick, whom I found to be the most amusing girl I had ever met. The next day I was walking down from Harvard Yard to Eliot House when I spotted Harry Sedgwick whom I knew. I told him that I had met a May Sedgwick the night before and that she was the most amusing girl I had ever met. I asked if she was related to him. He looked at me with astonishment and admitted that she was his elder sister. The message was clear. How could anyone find his sister amusing?

Not long after that Mrs. Roosevelt was scheduled to speak at Groton School and Sam Peabody and I decided to go out to hear her. I had a car and could provide the transportation. Sam asked if we could give a ride to his cousin, May Sedgwick, and I was delighted. A few weeks later Sam and May were going to help at a South Boston settlement house where May's mother had worked, and they invited me along. Afterwards we were then going to have tea with their elderly cousin. They warned me not to be surprised if she wanted to know exactly who my parents were. I was amused when she didn't ask who my parents were, because she already knew and asked about them.

May had gone to boarding school in Canada and then on to Radcliffe. Distracted by her coming-out year and Boston parties, she had flunked out of Radcliffe twice. But she had remained determined to go to college and managed to get accepted at Alabama State College for Women. After a year there studying hard and getting good marks she was accepted at Tufts. She was living at home and going to Tufts when her mother died unexpectedly in the summer of 1948. She continued to live at home, keeping her father company, which proved to be a very comfortable arrangement. However, she wanted her father to marry again and decided that he never would, if she were living at home. When she had the opportunity to share a house with her friends B Bartlett and Alice Mumford, she moved in with them. Her plan worked and her father married Emily Lincoln.

May's contact with FDR was much more extensive than mine had been, When FDR came to Groton for his son's graduation, all the Peabody grandchildren were lined up to clasp him by the hand. When it became May's turn, she asked the President how he liked his new swimming pool. The President told her she must come and swim in it. Later, when she and her mother did visit the White House, she slept in the Lincoln bedroom. In the morning, when she was looking for her breakfast, she passed an open door. In the room was FDR eating his breakfast in bed. He invited her in and told her to sit on the bed while he finished his meal, which she did.

May's father told this story of his stay in the White House. In the room in which he was staying was a desk with White House writing paper on it. He thought he would take a number of sheets for future correspondence. To his surprise he discovered that only the top sheet contained the White House address.

May and I saw more and more of each other as time went on and became engaged to be married. My parents came down from Auburn for an engagement party. They stayed at the Somerset Club, and May and I dined with them the night before the party. I told my father that the Sedgwicks, like the Osbornes, were Democrats. My father looked patient and asked, "What do you think I have been doing all this past week?" Clearly he had been researching the Sedgwicks.

My cousin Anne Chase and her husband Irving came to the engagement party. When I introduced them to Minturn Sedgwick, my future father-in-law, he smiled and said that he had met Anne before. He explained that he and my Uncle Bob had been in the same unit in World War I and that Anne had been in her crib when he visited her parents, Bob and Martha Osborne. May told me after the party that her grandfather, after he had met me, had greeted her with "Thank God, thank God." May had been attending Tufts and her grandfather had been terrified that she was going to get engaged to somebody from Tufts. When I met him he told me that he and my grandfather, T. M. Osborne, had attended Adams Academy and Harvard at the same time. He said that the last time he had seen my grandfather was when he was in TM's rooms and had accidentally knocked over an oil lamp. My grandfather had turned to him and said "Sedgwick, leave the room." When May called to tell her Aunt Mary of our engagement her aunt reacted by saying "But May, he's so handsome." The implication was how did May manage to land such a handsome man. May was most amused by the comment.

I missed my graduation because I was at Red Top, the Harvard crew's training camp on the Thames River opposite New London, Conn. The crews were at the camp for two weeks rowing twice a day every day, training for the Yale race. The race was located there as it was the only four-mile straight away on the East Coast. The varsity rowed four miles and the JVs and freshmen two miles. We swept the river that year, with our boat winning by more than a length.

May and I stayed with the Storrows at their summer place in Stonington that night and then drove to Dedham the next day. Then we headed back to Auburn, where I was to work at The Citizen until it was time for our wedding. The trip was also to give May an introduction to Auburn. On the way we stopped at Stockbridge to visit the Sedgwick House, built by Judge Sedgwick in 1784. Then we went to Deerfield to see my old school. Frank Boyden, the headmaster, was mildly pleased to see me, but delighted to be introduced to May. It turned out that Endicott Peabody, May's grandfather, and the founder of Groton School, had been friends with Mr. Boyden. They had roomed together at headmasters' conventions, and he recalled getting a telegram from Mrs. Peabody saying, "Make sure Cotty wears his rubbers." From Deerfield we went on to Willow Point where May was put in the guest room at the top of the stairs. She was told the evening train would be coming and did not think much about it. The next morning, she said that she heard the train coming and getting louder and louder and louder until she finally thought the conductor was going to ask her for her ticket.

Our marriage was set for August 26th in Murray Bay in the province of Quebec, where the Sedgwicks had a summer home. The bans were cried at May's church in Dedham, St. Peter's Church in Auburn, and in the Murray Bay Protestant Church, where the service was to take place. That church had been founded and was used by the summer visitors. (All the other churches in the area were Catholic.) Bishop Peabody, who was May's uncle, and the Rev. William Parsons, who was her cousin, officiated, as well as the rector of the church. My brother Richard was best man and Fan Sedgwick, May's sister, was maid of honor. May often recalled walking back down the aisle after the ceremony and looking at her family, all of whom were crying. Then she looked over at my family, all of whom were also crying. (They were all happy and moved by the ceremony.) After a reception at the Sedgwicks' house next to the church we drove to the Montgomery House next to Montmorency Falls outside of Quebec City. May had driven past the hotel for years without ever visiting it and had always wanted to stay there. We stayed at the Ritz in Montreal the next night and flew to Bermuda the next day.

As I was getting off the plane, I put my hand in my pocket and found my car keys. I had left the car at Montreal airport for Bill Hills, one of my ushers, to drive to Auburn. Happily, the plane was flying back to Montreal, so I gave the key to the pilot with instructions to leave it at the airline desk to be picked up. Then I called up the hotel where Bill was staying and left a message as to where the key could be recovered.

We stayed for the first few days at the Mid-Ocean Club and then at Fairwinds, the house my father and my Uncle Charles had inherited from their aunt, Helen Osborne Storrow. The house was on the ocean next to the golf course, with a beach and a tennis court. My Uncle Charles loved the house. My father did not, and later sold his interest to my uncle. After a two-week honeymoon, we flew to Boston, where I entered the Graduate School of Public Administration. May kept on teaching. We lived at 10 Trowbridge Street, a comfortable apartment not too far from the college, for the first half of the year. For the second half of the year, we shared a house in Lexington with Harry and Lennie Sedgwick. All the students at the graduate school were public servants who had been working for various public entities. I was the first person to go directly from college to the school. The curriculum consisted of graduate courses in government and economics. The work was hard, but I worked hard at it, much harder than I had in college, and I did quite well.

However, I did not feel I was learning anything which would be of much use to me in my future life. As a result, I applied and was accepted at the Harvard Business School. I had applied to the Business School the year before but had been turned down.

The Harry Sedgwicks had gone off to Geneva, Switzerland, where Harry was attending an Aluminium Co of Canada graduate school. As a result, we took an apartment at 72 Dana Street in Cambridge and shared it with an amiable Newfoundland dog and a cocker spaniel, both given to us. Dukie, the Newfoundland, was the first of a series of dogs, who have shared my life. He came to Auburn with us and enjoyed life at Grover Street and Willow Point. After Dukie died we inherited Devereaux, a mixed breed, from Lithgow. When he died, May was starting to feel poorly, and I decided not to replace him. I did miss having a dog, but my life was such that not replacing him was the wiser course. When I married Sheila, I welcomed her two dogs, Lilly and Bear. Then came Willow and finally Beau.

Work at the Business School was not as hard as the year before, but there was a great deal of it. A paper was due every week and there was a three-hour exam on most Saturday mornings. At the end of the school year my Uncle Charles announced, "that it was time I stopped fooling around Cambridge and went to work." Since I had worked very hard in graduate school, I did not consider that I had been "fooling around". However, I did not tell him that. Instead, May and I started making plans to settle in Auburn.

CHAPTER 14

Living in Auburn

We settled on a house at 40 Grover Street and made an offer of $14,000, which was accepted by the owner, Samuel Kennedy. He had been asking $16,000. He was deaf and it turned out that he had thought I had accepted his $16,000 price. We both stood firm on our figures and May and I started looking elsewhere. I was very taken by the house next door at 34 Grover Street. It was larger, with attractive rooms, a barn, and an ample backyard. We bought it for $21,000, paid for mostly by a gift of $10,000 from Minturn Sedgwick and a mortgage of $10,000. Our plans were to make an apartment on a portion of the second floor, which we did.

Before we took possession of the house the previous owner held an auction of much of its contents. May went to the auction with $1,000. The first thing she did was to buy a chair to sit in. After that she bought the stove, the refrigerator, the curtains, several beds, and a bureau. There was a painting of a couple on a porch which I particularly liked, and I asked May to buy it if it went for less than $100. May was the highest bidder at $75. (The picture still hangs in our sunroom and was later appraised at $750.)

When we set out to furnish the house, we were given furniture from Groton which had been stored since the Rector had retired. A mirror and a highboy came from the Sedgwick garage. Other sofas and chairs came from class-mates who were departing from Cambridge. Our bed was a gift from my father-in-law. My parents provided excess furniture from 99 including a fireplace surround which is still in our library. As a result of these kindnesses, we managed to furnish the whole house without buying anything new.

Over the years we were also given a number of paintings and purchased others. Some of the gifts came from May's family, some from mine, and some from friends. They include family portraits, a large number of landscapes, and some not very good modern abstract paintings. Four of the family portraits are of my mother. The rest are of ancestors three or more generations further back. One portrait of my mother had been put up for auction at Southby's Auction House in London. When it did not sell, I was able to buy it. The landscapes are mainly by Barney, Clough and Rising.

The original portion of the house had been built in 1828, partly by a Mormon, Brigham Young. Over the years two wings have been added, substantially increasing the size of the house. It was in good condition when we purchased it and we thought we would not have to make any changes. Little did we know. The first thing we did was to make an apartment out of the second-floor west wing. We rented out that apartment until our family grew large enough so that we needed the space. Over the course of years, we built an attached garage, enclosed the back and side porches, refinished the former kitchen in the basement, shut off the backstairs, moved the kitchen and the dining room to the east wing, and the library to the west wing, and finally added the sunroom in 1991. At one point we had a swimming pool in the backyard. We fenced in the whole backyard, because a city ordinance required pools to be fenced in. We discovered later that the fenced-in yard made it a splendid place for the dogs to play.

My great-great-grandmother had come to dinner at the Grover Street house in the 1840s and wrote that she overheard one elderly woman say to her neighbor "That's Martha Wright, she is a very dangerous woman." Apparently, the elderly woman felt that way because Martha was a suffragette, an abolitionist, a Quaker, a teetotaler, and a Republican. Martha was clearly amused by the description for she wrote her family to tell them that "she was a very dangerous woman."

Dorothy Wickendem, a *New Yorker* editor, wrote a book about her, called *The Agitators*.

CHAPTER 15

At Willow Point After The War

After the war I was relegated to the guest house at Willow Point, as Devens, Barbie and their children had taken over the wing that Richard, Devens, my nurse and I had formerly occupied. I did not mind as I was the sole occupant and quite comfortable. I was there by myself all during my college years. After my marriage May joined me, and, in time, our children and a babysitter. We would move out to the lake after the children finished school in the spring. On the first of August, we would go off to Murray Bay. May and the children would spend the month there and I would spend as much time as my vacation allowed.

Greve Raben.
(Raben-Levetzau)

Painting of Lillie by her sister, Suzanne

Devens, Erik, and Richard

Erik and Lillie playing backgammon when he had rheumatic fever

Willow Point in 2021

Ditchley, home of Ronnie and Marietta Peabody Tree

Elizabeth who missed out on a dance with Erik

The original "99" before it was reduced in size

Devens, Richard, Lithgow, Erik, Lillie

Erik at Aalholm with Jackdaws

Erik rowing at an early age

Willow Point in the 1930s

Erik's children: Lucretia, Minturn, Lithgow, Betsey, Sally, Christopher, and Sam at Catherine Lange's wedding at Willow Point

Willow Point when the ice went out one year, and pushed a 500 lb stone 10 feet in the air

Aalholm Slot (castle), Lillie's home in Nysted, Denmark was purchased from the King in 1725 and was built in 1375

May and Erik

Sheila and Erik

Sheila and Erik's wedding in 2002

Sam and Eleanor Osborne

110

Sandra and Christopher Osborne

Bob and Sally Edgar

Betsey Osborne and Madeleine Stein

Lithgow Osborne and Chuck Burleigh

Minturn Osborne

Jonathon and Lucretia Wells

At Willow Point the children would swim, play in the brook, sail, play tennis, or explore the woods. May and I ate every night with my parents, while the children were fed by the babysitter.

I had a variety of sailboats—dinghies, sunfish, sailfish and finally a Flying Scot, which was larger and had a jib and a mainsail. (That boat was christened William Jones. This was in honor of a man from whom I had won $1,000 at backgammon one night, thereby enabling me to buy the boat.)

When the children grew older, I would organize treasure hunts for them. The clues were hidden all over the property and the children would go from one clue to another. I started out having two teams but that proved to be too complicated. As a result, I changed to one team and a trip to Deedee's ice cream parlor outside Moravia. The clues were all in plain sight. Some of the clues I used are shown below.

- Named for she who said, "Speak for Yourself John."
- A speedometer for a stationary object.
- This looks the same from either side.

- Red assassins fear T-Men.
- Go to a place where love means nothing.
- This is an alternate power play.

The answers are at the end of the book.

On weekends Dev and Barbie would come down from Rochester with their children. He had started working at Eastman Kodak after his graduation from the University of Arizona. He had a speed boat, and his friends would come out on Sundays for a picnic and water skiing. We would sit on the end of the point, eat our luncheons, and watch as our friends tried out the skis. One day Dr. Ralph Getty fell off the skis just by the end of the point and was wildly floundering in the water. He appeared to be in serious trouble, so I swam out to him and pulled him to shore. He was very grateful. My father was an avid salmon fisherman and would rent the fishing rights on a Canadian river for a week each year if he could schedule a trip. I went with him three times, once before the war and twice after I had started working for the newspaper. The first time I went, was to Anticosti Island in the middle of the St. Lawrence. The stream was small, and you could see the salmon in the stream. I would cast beyond the fish and then pull the fly in front of him, hoping he would take the fly. Once hooked you had to play the fish until he tired. Then you could pull him close enough to shore so that the guide could net him. If you did not play the fish carefully, he would be apt to tear loose from the hook. I had to play one salmon for forty-five minutes before he could be netted.

The other two times I went fishing were less fun. The streams were bigger, and you could not see the fish. I found casting and getting no bites and not knowing if there were any fish in the stream very frustrating.

CHAPTER 16
Hunting in South Carolina

Christian Herter, my father's college roommate, had married a Standard Oil heiress, Mary Caroline (Mac) Pratt, whose family owned a 6,000-acre hunting plantation near Beaufort, SC. If the family was not using it, they would invite my father and members of his family to hunt there. It was great fun. We would get on the sleeper in New York and be met at a station not too far from the plantation the next morning. The plantation consisted of a very comfortable living room, dining room and kitchen in one house and sleeping quarters in an adjoining building. Every morning the maids would come in to light a fire in each room. We would dress and be served our breakfast in the other building. After we had eaten the huntsman would come in and discuss what part of the plantation we would be hunting in that day. When that was determined, we read or played chess until the horses were brought around. We would mount up and ride out to the area we were going to hunt. A man-servant would have driven out, set up a table, and chairs, and laid out our lunch. After lunch we would mount up and the dogs would be turned loose. We would follow them on horseback until one of the dogs went on point. Then two of us would dismount, hand the reins to a groom, get out our shotguns, and walk up behind the dogs. Nothing would happen until there was a whoosh and about twenty quail would get up all at once. If you are a good shot, you could hit two birds, one from each barrel. If you were not a good shot, you could miss with both barrels. I missed a lot of quail. The huntsman, who managed the dogs, would spot the birds which had not flown too far. We would walk up on them and shoot at them as they got up. That done, we would go in search of another covey. We would find four or five coveys in an afternoon. When the hunting was done, we would ride back to the house. There was no telephone or television in our quarters. It was a great vacation.

CHAPTER 17
Working at The Citizen

When May and I moved back to Auburn from Cambridge, I went to work at the newspaper, first working in the press room. I then sold classified advertising for a while until I took the place of a reporter who was leaving. As a reporter I covered all the various beats at one time or another—city hall, the county office building, police and the Farm and Home Bureau. I was paid the same amount as the other reporters in the newsroom for the three years I worked as a reporter.

I recall one time when I was covering Recorder's Court a Mohawk Indian was brought in on a charge of being drunk. He was very short and very broad. He was on his way to his reservation from New York City where he had been working on skyscraper construction. (The Mohawks had great balance and no fear of heights and had found a niche in skyscraper construction.) The judge told him if on his honor as a Mohawk Indian, he would promise never to come back to Auburn, he would let him go. The Indian promised and was on his way back to the reservation.

While I was on the police beat, we received a call that a woman had been found dead near Port Byron. Verne Moe, the photographer, and I went out to the house. It was the most depressing place I had ever seen. It was a mess. Papers and clothing were strewn all over. Recently opened food tins were piled in one corner. A crib stood against one wall. It turned out that a young unmarried couple had lived there with their new baby. The father had been killed in a railroad accident some weeks before and the mother had committed suicide. It was one of the most depressing sights I have ever seen.

When Alan Goodfader, the city editor, left I asked for and was given his job and my pay went up. As city editor I oversaw all the local news and had three reporters working for me.

I assigned the beat reporters, edited their stories, and wrote the headlines. I worked under Chuck Wellner, who wrote the editorials and had total charge of the news operations. The sports editor worked under me and handled the local and national sports news, selecting the stories, writing, and editing the copy and writing the headlines. The wire editor also worked under me. He selected the stories from the Associated and United Press, wrote the headlines for them and laid out the front page.

We carried all local weddings accounts if they were provided to us. I realized one day that we were carrying no pictures or stories of Black weddings. The next time a Black minister came into the office I asked him why this was. I will never forget what he said. He told me "We assumed that you would not carry Black weddings, so we never sent them in." I told him we would carry all local weddings, Black or white, and to pass the word along. He did and we covered Black weddings from then on.

Ours was an evening paper. We had a three o'clock news deadline after which a story would have to be held until the next day. Then it would be old news, already covered by the Syracuse morning paper.

We had a very firm news policy. If it was local news about local people, we carried the story no matter who it was or if they asked us not to. This policy included members of the Osborne family. Such a policy made us few friends, but we were never sued. Because our policy was so firm and so long-standing, we had few requests from people trying to keep their names out of the paper. We did tread very carefully where possible libel was concerned.

When Jim Converse, Barbie Osborne's father, shot and killed a man in a drunken moment, and went to jail, we carried the story. We could probably have ignored the story, since it took place in Arizona, but we followed our policy. Also, when my father sued my Uncle Charles's estate over the value of the *Citizen*, we covered the court story extensively until the matter was finally resolved.

When May and I started living in Auburn we had my salary, and the money May received from running a nursery school in our house. We also received some money from her mother's trust fund and some from my grandfather's estate. We also had the rent from the apartment. We were incredibly careful with what we spent and did not have to ask our parents for money even as the children started arriving.

In 1954, Minturn Sedgwick became concerned about the dangerous effects of smoking. As a result, he offered May, Harry, and Fan $500 each if they would give up smoking for a year and fifty dollars a year thereafter if they would continue not smoking. We were always in need of money and May did not hesitate a minute. She had been smoking a pack a day since she was sixteen, but she gave it up and never smoked again. She collected those fifty-dollar payments until her father died.

As far as I can remember we never told our children not to smoke. But we did say, in front of them, that smoking was silly, unhealthy, dirty, and expensive and that people who smoked were stupid. They seem to have gotten the message because none of them smokes today. In May's case the damage was done, as she died of lung cancer at the age of seventy-two. I tried one cigarette when I was at Deerfield and did not like it and never tried another. Up to that time I had stayed away from smoking because I was an enthusiastic but not particularly good athlete, and I thought that smoking would only make me worse.

When our children were old enough, we sent them to a nursery school at the Westminster

Presbyterian Church. I would pick up whoever was attending the school on my way home for lunch. I had a seat on the back of the bicycle and my child would sit in that. My children would chatter away as I cycled. As the child was invisible to pedestrians coming towards us, the pedestrians would think that I was the one talking. We startled people that way. While I was city editor, I had one of my few experiences in public speaking. George Shamon, who was a friend, was Auburn's corporation counsel. He was also president of the Corporation Counsels Association of New York State. The custom was for the association to hold its summer meeting in the city of the president. George was making the dinner arrangements and asked me to address the final dinner. I suspect he had asked others and had been turned down. At any rate I settled down to write my speech.

May and I went to dinner, which was at Krebs. It was preceded by a cocktail party which lasted an hour and a half. This was followed by a three course Krebs dinner which included roast beef and potatoes. After the dinner ended, I was called on to speak. I looked at my audience, and could see that they were drunk, glassy-eyed and about to fall asleep. I made an instant decision. I abandoned my thoughtful 10-minute speech, welcomed them to Auburn, thanked them for their public service and sat down. My action was greeted with enthusiastic applause. After seven years on the news desk, I felt I should become more involved in the business end of the newspaper and told my Uncle Charles and Bill Dapping that I wanted to be assistant general manager.

They had run the paper very successfully for a good many years, including outselling the opposition Advertiser Journal and later buying it. For about ten years they ran both papers, the *Citizen* with a Democratic slant and the *Advertiser-Journal* with a Republican slant. During the depression they merged the two papers. They had also bought radio station WMBO, the only radio station in town. But in recent years they had not kept up with the times. They were making money and were quite content with things as they were. They were somewhat surprised by my request but did agree to give me the job.

At that time the Auburn Publishing Company owned both the *Citizen-Advertiser* and WMBO-AM and FM. My Uncle Charles owned a majority of the stock in the company, given to him by his father. Bill Dapping and my father had minority interests as well as some other people, who had very small interests. My father and Dapping had a legal agreement with my uncle that they could buy his shares from his estate for $25 a share. As the value of newspapers in general went up my uncle grew unhappy with the arrangement. He wanted the stock price increased. My father consented to a price increase to $30 a share but balked at a second request. This whole arrangement was awkward for me. If my father died before my uncle, he would be free to sell to whomever he wished, and I might be out of a job. The valuation issue was finally settled by agreeing that Ernst & Ernst, our accountants, would decide the price.

When Uncle Charles died in 1961, Ernst & Ernst said that they would not decide on the value of the stock, as valuations of this sort were not in their purview. The estate's response was to set the stock price at $60 a share. My father refused this price and a lawsuit threatened. I called Bob Erskine, a New York lawyer and a friend from Deerfield, Harvard, and the

Spee Club. He found an independent appraiser who set the price at $45 a share. The estate rejected this price, and my father started a lawsuit. On the courthouse steps the estate offered to accept the $45 price. My father and Joe Lynch, our lawyer, felt we had a good case but left it up to me to decide whether to accept the price or continue the lawsuit. I made the decision to go ahead with the suit, a decision which I feel in retrospect was a vast and stupid mistake. After a painful court case the judge set the price at $45. This decision was upheld on appeal to two higher courts, and we won the case. If I had accepted the offer, we would have avoided a very difficult family dispute, lawyer's fees and worrisome uncertainty and could have started running the paper three years sooner. I had always been good friends with my cousin Agnes, but not after the court case.

I continued to work at the paper while the court case was being heard. It was an awkward position to be in, but I did have a job and continued to work at it. My father, who was vice president of the company, was fired. He filed for unemployment and collected a few checks. He stopped collecting them when collecting them interfered with a proposed salmon fishing trip. While I had a job as long as Agnes was running the paper, I realized that if she won the lawsuit, she would probably sell the paper and I would be out of a job. I decided I should finish working for my master's degree by going to Syracuse University. I took evening classes and wrote a thesis titled "The Problems of A Boss's Son in a Family-Owned Business" I sent out questionnaires to everybody I knew, who was in that situation. Their answers were the basis for my thesis. When I had to defend my thesis one of the professors said dismissively that the thesis was like a magazine article. I thought that was a compliment. At any rate I was awarded my master's degree in business administration.

When we took over the newspaper, we arranged to exchange Bill Dapping's stock for bonds, which were to be left to Syracuse University, Wells College, and Harvard. We also bought up the shares of all the outside stockholders until all the stock was held by the Lithgow Osborne family. My father gave most of his shares to my brothers, to me and to my nieces and nephews. I also bought other shares from him with the result that I wound up with control of the company.

We fired Chuck Wellner and had Sam Kennedy write the editorials and supervise the newsroom. My father left me with overall management of the company and wrote editorials when the spirit moved him. We started promotions in the circulation and classified advertising departments and began planning for a new building. My Uncle Charles had done very little to increase circulation and we were able to up the daily circulation from 13,000 to 20,000 by adding rural routes in Cayuga County and elsewhere and by adding a reporter to cover news in Skaneateles. When we acquired the newspaper the single copy price was seven cents, and the weekly price was forty-two cents. One day I noticed a cigarette machine which was selling packages of cigarettes for fifty cents. I thought if people pay 50 cents for a pack of cigarettes, they will certainly pay more for a newspaper. The next day we raised the single copy price to ten cents and the weekly price to fifty cents and hoped we would not lose too many readers. The results were very satisfying. We did not lose any subscribers. On the other hand, the *Herald-Journal*, the Syracuse afternoon paper, did lose subscribers. The reason for this was that a number of people had been taking both papers and dropped the one they found less interesting to save money.

We built a new plant and converted the newspaper to offset printing. The new press enabled us to cut production costs. The visual quality of the paper was also improved. We were constantly receiving inquiries from companies wishing to buy the newspaper. A major portion of the family's money was invested in the *Citizen*, and we had a very handsome profit from our investment. I agonized about what to do. I was happy running the newspaper, but I recognized it was a risky and fragile investment. It was not a venture into which one should put all his money. A strike could shut us down completely. If another newspaper was started in town, it might drain all our profits. These were the kind of risks that were keeping me awake at night. I finally decided that the right thing to do was to sell. My father agreed and I started looking. The best offer came from the Ingersoll newspapers. We made a deal with them and sold at a substantial profit. My father retired and I became the publisher of the paper for the Ingersolls. I really didn't enjoy working for them, but not enough to quit. Ralph Ingersoll 2nd, with whom I dealt, insisted on some operational changes, but not many. He did feel that we should be making more money.

After I had been working for Ingersoll for two years, I received a stunning shock. I was told that the Ingersolls had sold the paper and that the new owners, another newspaper chain, had their own publisher. I was out of my job. Of course, Auburn Cablevision still employed me. I took my grandfather's desk and departed from the building I had helped to design and build. It was a very difficult time. It was also wrenching to see some of the women in the office crying as I walked out of the office. I still use my grandfather's desk today.

In retrospect I was right in my decision to sell the paper. With the advent of the internet the newspaper business changed for the worse. The paper's print circulation, which was 20,000 copies daily when the paper was sold, is now 3,800. The digital circulation is another 5,789. The newstand price when we sold the paper was 10 cents. Now it is two dollars, which suggests why the circulation has fallen so sharply. Classified advertising, which was more than a page, is almost entirely gone as is display advertising.

I was offered and accepted a job teaching a graduate class in newspaper management at the Newhouse School of Journalism at Syracuse University. It was an error. And it went very badly. I had no curriculum and had to design my own from week to week. I had trouble keeping my students straight. I quit after one term.

CHAPTER 18

Radio and Cable

WMBO-AM had been purchased in the 1930s when the original owner had run into financial difficulties. It was profitable, but not very profitable and had been acquired more as an insurance policy than anything else. When frequency modulation (FM) became available, I, with my radar background, urged my uncle and Bill Dapping to get an FM license, which they did. Our FM signal was a strong one and covered all the area between Auburn and Rochester. Because of the location of the tower in Scipio the signals did not reach Syracuse. We carried the same programming on both stations. In those days a different radio set was required to pick up FM signals. As the radio sets became able to carry both AM and FM signals, we initiated separate programming for the FM station. At one time we carried the Family Rosary for Peace for the Roman Catholic Diocese of Rochester as we were the only station capable of reaching the whole diocese.

I became nervous about owning a newspaper, radios stations and a cable system in the same market. Would it be considered a monopoly? I didn't know. Anyhow we decided to sell WMBO AM and FM. After WMBO was sold the new owner put up a booster tower on the east side of Owasco Lake, which enabled the FM station to reach the Syracuse market. I wish I had thought of that. In retrospect I think I was overly concerned about the monopoly considerations. I think the FCC had more important issues to worry about. We launched an FM station, WMAX, in 1992 in the Rochester area using an alternate rock format. It was a Class A FM station licensed to Irondequoit and covering the Rochester market. In 1996, we made a deal with George Kimble, an area radio station operator, for a second station, WMIX, a Class A FM station licensed to Brighton. As a result, we became the first company in New York State to have two stations in one market. My son Minturn worked for the radio stations, which did very nicely. In 1997 we sold those two stations and a "repeater station" (also a Class A FM station serving the Rochester market, which carried WMAX programming to another part of the region). The buyer was a group operator, Jacor Broadcasting, and the price was $7,500,000. We used some of the proceeds to pay Kimble for his station and to pay off the loan we had taken out to rebuild the Auburn Cablevision plant. A portion of the remaining funds was distributed to cable's stockholders.

With the advent of television, station licenses had been granted to Syracuse operators by the Federal Communications Commission and we were concerned about what would happen to WMBO. We could not get into the television business because stations were expensive to launch, and we knew nothing about the television business. The radio business did change but it survived quite nicely. Then one day our paper carried a story that a company named Meredith-Avco had applied for a franchise to build a cable television system in Auburn.

I had no idea what cable television was,

but I soon learned. When television had first started viewers who lived in valleys were unable to receive station signals. This problem was solved by building towers, which could receive the signals. These signals were then carried by cable to viewers' homes for a fee. In the beginning cable television existed only in communities where residents could not receive television signals off the air. Then cable operators in New York State found they could pick up the signals of the three New York City non-network stations and carry these signals by microwave to their systems. These three stations were popular enough that viewers with off-the-air service were prepared to pay for cable. This was so, because their programs differed and competed against NBC, CBS, and ABC in New York City.

Should we go into the cable television business? I remembered a Harvard Business School professor saying that the railroads thought they were in the railroad business when they were actually in the transportation business. Consequently, they missed out on the bus, trucking, and airline businesses. I thought "we are in the communications business, and we should be in the cable television business too." The Auburn City Council gave us a franchise to operate a cable television system, but also gave one to General Electric, which had a plant in Auburn. We went into negotiations with General Electric and later Time-Warner to be partners in an Auburn cablevision venture. They both seemed interested but proved to be terribly slow moving. While we were talking to them, we found that the New York Telephone Company would build a cable system and lease it to us for ten years. This would eliminate the large capital investment required to build a cable system ourselves.

We located a tower site, received permission to carry the NYC stations and started building a facility to process the signals. While we were doing this General Electric was doing nothing with its franchise. Finally, we decided that we were so far ahead of General Electric that they would hesitate to try to overbuild us, and that we did not need them as partners. It was a scary decision for us to make considering our relative sizes, but we held our breath and went ahead. GE did nothing, with the result that we were the owners of the only operating cable television system in Auburn. The first year we lost $100,000 and the second year

$175,000 but the business continued to grow. Indeed, in the whole time we owned the cable system there was only one month when gross revenues were less than the previous month.

I was president of the company, dealing with franchises, financing, program selections and deciding company policies. As the years went on, we added HBO, CineMax, CNN, ESPN, some local programing, local ads, and a host of other channels, and we were serving 14,000 subscribers. We were grossing $500,000 in local advertising revenue at almost no expense.

Rita Valentino was the general manager and looked after day-to-day operations and did so very well. I used to say that before she spent a nickel the Indian was riding the buffalo. I recall one time when she wanted a raise, she asked me if I thought I could run cable without her. I was taken aback and thought for several minutes before replying. I told her "Rita, I have no desire to run cable without you, but, yes, I think I would be able to manage." That ended that conversation, but we later did agree to take equal salaries.

When we started out, we were carrying the ABC, CBS and NBC stations from both Syracuse and Rochester, the three NYC independents and a Canadian tv channel. We also had a local time-weather channel on which we could do local programming and carry ad messages. The substantial change came when Ted Turner, who owned a UHF station in Atlanta, realized he could send his station's signal up to a satellite and thence down to cable systems all across the country. He carried the Atlanta Braves, and the service was an instant hit. He followed that with Cable News Network (CNN) which featured 24-hour news. We carried both channels, although I thought CNN's cost of gathering the news would be prohibitive. I was quite wrong about its viability. Turner made arrangements with television stations across the country to feed him news and managed very well indeed.

As the cable television industry grew and prospered it was dominated by major operators who had millions of subscribers in thousands of communities and were buying up the smaller systems left and right. In addition to television services, they were offering telephone and internet services. I doubted that we had the technical skills to provide the same services. With the advent of the internet it became possible to use the internet to stream television programs. I worried about the possibility that one of the big companies would overbuild us and offer a broader range of services.

Also, the Teamsters union had organized our employees and was proving difficult at times. I had tried to negotiate with them but found it impossible. To solve the problem, we hired a labor relations law firm to do the negotiating. While our labor costs went up, we were still able to operate profitably. (Our employees never did threaten to strike us, but with the Teamsters that possibility always lurked in the background.)

Also we received very, very generous purchase offers from some of the larger cable companies. Cable systems at that time were selling for $2,000 a subscriber and we had 14,000 subscribers. With some reluctance I decided to sell. The company was owned by me and my children, and by other members of the Osborne family. When we did sell in 1998, I was left with a considerable amount of money and no job. For the first time in my life, I had no office to go to. The rest of the stockholders, who were not working for the company, were quite happy with an unexpected windfall.

I should note that sometime after the sale

our former employees did go on strike. The new owners hired scabs and ran the company successfully for a year after which they hired replacement employees. I am glad I did not have to face a strike situation. Some years later I ran into Paul Bush, the Teamster business agent with whom I had had to deal. He told me that he had urged the employees not to go on strike, but that they had been adamant. He said that he had not been able to talk them out of striking.

Also, Spectrum, which now owns the Auburn system, has competition from Verizon, which streams television signals over its internet wires. I am sure we would have had competition from Verizon as well. Television signals being transmitted via the internet as well as by cable or over the air has led to an incredible increase in the number of television signals available to viewers. Sadly, after selling Cable I made some bad investments, which reduced the profit from the Cablevision sale.

CHAPTER 19

Labor Unions

The thing I disliked most during my career in business was dealing with labor unions. Although none of them ever mentioned the word "strike" to me, it was always lurking in the back of my mind. A strike could have shut down the newspaper and made life very difficult at cablevision. Group operators were in a far better position to cope with strikes and were generally able to continue operating. I doubt if we could have done so in the case of the newspaper.

A group in our newsroom contacted the American Newspaper Guild, which represented news and advertising employees in most of the larger newspapers. The National Labor

Relations Board held an election in which the guild was defeated, I think mainly by the votes of the business office, advertising, and circulation departments. I was vastly relieved as the guild had the reputation of being a very difficult union.

Composing room employees were represented by the International Typographical Union (ITU) and had been for years. Press room employees were represented by the press room union. I negotiated with both unions and was always able to settle new contracts. The jurisdictional divisions as to who would do what work were always clear until we started building the new building and planning for a new offset press. The offset process required a large camera to create a page negative. Both unions felt that their members should be handling the camera. We felt the more efficient procedure was to have the press crew handle the camera. The design of the building depended on where the camera would be located. All parties finally agreed that the camera would be in the composing room and that the page negative would be lowered through a slot in the floor to the press room. (The Citizen is no longer printed in Auburn.

It is printed in the plant of the Canandaigua Messenger and trucked to Auburn.)

At Auburn Cablevision I received a telegram one day announcing that my employees had decided to join the Teamsters Union. It was a bolt out of the blue. I had no idea that the employees felt they needed union representation. After one meeting with the Teamster representative, I realized that I was in over my head, and we hired a Washington law firm that specialized in union negotiations. Peter Carre, the lawyer sent by the law firm, provided a bulwark, and managed to negotiate a contract with which we could live. In retrospect the Teamsters were far more difficult to deal with than the ITU or the Press union. I always felt that the Teamsters thought of themselves first, the employees second and the company third. They insisted on their pension and health plans, which were not as good as the ones we had in place. The union was one of the reasons I sold the company when I did.

CHAPTER 20

After Cable

In the 1980s I invested in two Broadway productions for reasons which now escape me. The first was a musical about Victoria Woodhull, a noted feminist and lady stockbroker, who was the first woman to run for president. The show ran for only one performance. The second production was a British play called "Pack of Lies", about spies in London. It had been a great success in England, running for nearly a year, featuring Judy Dench and winning awards, and later being made into a movie. In view of its London success, I thought it would do well in New York. It was not to be. It closed after 120 performances.

After I sold the cable system, I was spending

more time in New York City. One day, when I was getting off the subway, the duffle bag I was carrying was caught in the subway's closing doors. I was able to yank the bag free, but the incident set me to thinking about writing a children's book. Supposing a little girl was carrying her favorite doll, and it was caught in the closing subway doors and was whisked away by the subway train. I started planning what might have happened to that doll. I imagined a variety of adventures for the doll and then finally its safe return to her owner. After writing the book I was able to get Hetty Tehan, a Skaneateles artist, to do the illustrations to go with the story. She did a wonderful job, portraying the characters just as I had imagined them. Then I found a firm that would print the book. I still consider *The Adventures of Tilly* my best effort.

I had started to write a murder mystery, *Murder on the Hill*, in the 1980s, but had abandoned it after May read what I had written and was most dismissive. I had used a typewriter and found that corrections and changes were very difficult. After I finished *Tilly*, I had the unfinished *Murder on the Hill* manuscript put in my computer and was able to finish the book to my satisfaction. My daughter Sally had her husband Bob pose as the corpse for the cover and I had the book printed. Sheila found the book difficult to follow and did not finish it. I was amused that both my wives had objections to the book.

I then edited and had printed Minturn Sedgwick's memoirs and later my father's diary of his time in Berlin during World War One. I titled that *Wandering into World War One*. Since then, I have also written three short novels, *Taking Fortune's Tide*, *Finding the Pot of Gold*, and *Marooned in Eden*. They are now available on Amazon, and I get royalties from time to time.

One thing which I found interesting about my father's diary is that he was clearly in favor of going to war with Germany. A few years before his death the subject arose, and he said he thought going to war with Germany in 1917 had been a mistake. He felt if the Europeans had been left to themselves, they would have fought until they were utterly exhausted and then ended the war with a more reasonable treaty. Such a treaty, he felt, would have prevented Hitler.

After spending ten years of my life writing

or editing newspaper stories it was fun to move on to fiction. One doesn't have to worry about facts when you are writing fiction. If the facts don't suit you, you change them. Thanks to the wonders of the computer, it is now possible to create a presentable book at very little expense. I have been pleased with the results. Another small pleasure I have is listing my occupation. Now, instead of listing "Retired" I list "Author".

CHAPTER 21

Life in Murray Bay

May had spent every summer of her life in Murray Bay, in a house on the shore of the St. Lawrence River downstream from the city of Quebec. The house had been built by Minturn Sedgwick's grandparents, Robert and Suzanne Shaw Minturn, and left to him by his grandmother when she died. Minturn's second wife, Emily Ames Lincoln, did not enjoy Murray Bay, so they had bought a house on Cape Cod. As a result Minturn gave the Murray Bay house to May, Harry and Fan, his older children. We would rent out the house in July and vacation there every August. May had lots of friends in the summer community, many of whom she had known since childhood. Life was a round of tennis, picnics, cocktail parties, and dinners.

Harry and Fan, each of whom owned a third of the house, would come less frequently, Harry sometimes with his children and sometimes not. Sadly, the time came when Harry and Fan were short of money and wanted to sell. Fan remarked that she was tired of paying for our summer vacations. May and I did not want to sell. I left the sale decision to May, and she reluctantly gave in. When we took a cab to go down to the NYC lawyer's office to sign the papers she was almost in tears. I told her that she did not have to sign the papers if she really, really didn't want to sell. She looked at me and said "if I don't sign Harry and Fan will never speak to me again." My response was "Well, would that be all bad?" That thought cheered her up enough so that she went ahead and signed.

The next two summers we stayed crowded in a cabin located on what was formerly the Sedgwick property. It was less than ideal, and we were very uncomfortable. In prior years May's grandfather had slept there and used it as a study. After looking at several houses we settled on one that was less than perfect. It belonged to Cammie Ross and was part of a large tract containing the houses of Cammie's relatives. I had agreed on a price of $35,000 Canadian with her father and offered a down payment which he said was unnecessary. I came home from tennis the next afternoon to be told by May that Cammie had called up to say that her son was very upset at the thought of selling the house. As a result, she had decided not to sell. As we were all friends, we decided not to press the claim that we already had an agreement to buy the house. Instead, we started to look elsewhere. In retrospect I was very, very grateful for Cammie's decision, for we ended up with a much nicer house. Later she did sell the house.

What we found was a larger, more handsome house with seven acres, a pond, and a tennis court. We bought it for $50,000. It had been built in 1903 by Richard Harlan, whose brother, Supreme Court Justice John Harlan, had built the house next door. The two houses shared a driveway. The house could hold all our children. One could barely see the river from the house as the view was blocked by trees. But I knew a beautiful view was available behind those trees and I went to work cutting them down. The result was a spectacular, panoramic view across the bay and down the St. Lawrence. When the house next door was sold its new owner told me he was so taken by the view that he bought the house without going inside it.

Our house was big enough to take care of all seven children and have room for some guests too. We had a cook and a caretaker, Edward Bergeron, who saw to it that the grass was mowed, and the tennis court was rolled every morning.

The year-around residents were all French-Canadian and spoke little English, so we had to struggle with the servants in French as best we could. May's French was far better than mine, so she did most of the running of the household. Eduard did speak some English, so I was able to communicate with him. The main part of the living room was two stories high and stretched across the whole front of the house. The dining table was in the southwest corner of the room next to the door to the pantry. The table had leaves and could seat fourteen if necessary. If we had that large a party the cook could always find someone to help serve.

Our trips to Murray Bay were never easy. At peak they consisted of May, me, seven children, the babysitter, and the dog. Staying at a motel was too expensive and too complicated so we tried camping, which was also too complicated. The final solution was to start out after work, put the children "to bed" at Watertown and drive all night. The children slept and May and I took turns driving. We were very tired the next day, but it still seemed the best solution. I put a large oblong sheet of plywood across the back of the station wagon two feet above the floor. Some of the children slept on the floor and the rest on the plywood. These days when the children want to amaze their friends, they tell of those trips. One of my memories of Murray Bay was a trip down the Murray River which I took with Sam and Christopher in an inflatable rubber raft. May drove us to a launching spot up the river and we arranged that she would pick us up at a spot just above the pulp mill dam.

The trip started out being great fun. We spotted a moose on the shore and passed a beaver dam in a small stream. There were occasional rapids, which were exciting when we dashed through them. But as time went on, I realized that the trip was taking much longer than I had anticipated. Darkness fell and we were still floating down the river unable to see what lay ahead. I was terrified that there might be a waterfall. I hoped I would be able to hear it before it was too late. A dark and now foreboding forest lay on either side of the stream. I did not want to go on and I did not want to struggle through the forest in the dark.

Finally, there seemed to be a road next to the stream. I decided to take my chance and we went ashore and clambered up the bank. To my immense relief there was a road. We walked down the road and eventually came to the spot where we were to meet May. She was not there. That was not surprising, since it was about nine o'clock. We kept walking up out of the river valley until we finally came to a house. I knocked on the door, asked to use the telephone, and called May. I could hear the relief in her voice when I told her we were fine. She came and picked us up. I drove out and picked up the raft the next day.

May and I competed most years in the tennis tournaments put on by the Manoir Richelieu hotel and Murray Bay Golf Club. We were runners-up at least six times but were never able to win the mixed doubles. I did win the men's doubles three times with three different partners. As I grew older, I would play every morning with my next-door neighbor, Philippe de Montebello. He would appear at 10 AM sharp every morning with a new can of tennis balls and we would play for about an hour and a half. Eventually as I grew older, he began to beat me more and more easily. One day as we were resting while changing sides, I suggested that he might want to find a more challenging partner. He said "No, it is good for my ego." I told him "That he certainly didn't need anything to boost his ego." He laughed and said he supposed that was true.

I also played chess with Philippe. I bought a chess clock, and we enjoyed battles across the chess board. He eventually stopped playing when his son Mark became so good that he could go into the other room and play with each of us without a board and beat both of us.

Later I played backgammon with August Chouquette. He would appear in the afternoon, and we would play for a couple of hours. In the beginning he was a steady source of income. As time went on, he grew better, and we were playing about even when I sold the house in 2011.

Murray Bay was not the same after May

died. She adored it as the high point of her year. She felt as if she were coming home. She could see her childhood friends and visit picnic spots filled with happy memories. I enjoyed Murray Bay, but I was also attached to Willow Point, my childhood home, which I had inherited from my father. The roof of the Murray Bay house was leaking, and the foundations were starting to rot. I agonized for some time about what to do. Finally, I decided two summer places was one too many, so I put the Murray Bay house on the market in 2011. I thought it would take a long time to sell. To my surprise I received an offer the day after I put it on the market. The offer was nine times what I had paid for the house and far, far more than I had expected. I have always told myself that the favorable price was due to all the work I had done to clear the view. My belief is validated by the fact that the new owners tore the house down and built a new one on the site.

CHAPTER 22

Life in New York City

ay had always yearned for an apartment in New York City and we entered into negotiations to buy an apartment being built on Roosevelt Island, formerly Welfare Island. When we found that the apartment came with a substantial mortgage, we told the sellers we were not interested. At about this time Fan Sedgwick moved from New York to Washington, leaving her apartment vacant. It was a very nice apartment, but the rent was substantial. We used that apartment until Bob and Sally Edgar decided to move from their apartment on 90th street to something larger. Their apartment was small and rather dark but suitable for a pied-a-terre. We stayed there until 1990 when we were offered an apartment on 12th Street owned by Alan Johnson, Sam's father-in-law. This apartment turned out to be uncomfortable and to have very uncertain heating. Consequently, when we were offered the chance to buy an apartment at the Osborne, a cooperative apartment building on 57th Street and Seventh Avenue, we decided to take it. As the Osborne was a cooperative, we had to appear before the cooperative's board to be approved before the sale could be finalized. We gave Marietta Tree and Congressman Ham Fish as our references. May was worried that we would not get board approval. I was not. We were seated on a dais facing about ten people. As far as I can remember, the questions we were asked were neither searching nor unfriendly and we were approved as residents.

We never used any of the apartments very much. We would drive down from Auburn so that I could attend meetings of the board of the Osborne Association or confer with my lawyers and my accountants. The trips also gave me a chance to play backgammon at the Harvard Club and the Racquet Club and to see some plays and our NYC friends and relations. The Osborne apartment was located on the first floor and looked out on an air shaft. The heating was less than perfect, at times too hot and at times too cold. I decided to sell it. The broker found a buyer who was prepared to buy it at a profit to me, and I was very pleased. Then Osborne's cooperative board turned the prospective buyer down and we went back to square one. However, a man named Robert Osborn, who lived at the Osborne, wanted a place where his guests could stay, and offered to buy our apartment at a modest profit to me. Since he was already a resident there was no problem with the cooperative's board and the deal went through. Robert Osborn worked for Turner Classic Movies television channel introducing their movies. He turned out to be a very pleasant man and we were both amused that an apartment at the Osborne was being sold by an Osborne to an Osborn.

I purchased a very nice apartment on 94th Street which was located on the fifth floor and had a view of a school playground across the street. I discovered that Fifth Avenue, a block to the west, had a never-ending stream of empty taxicabs coming down from Harlem. However, Sheila and I eventually found that we were not using it enough to justify keeping it.

As a result, we sold it in 2005 to our friends the Donaldsons for their son in medical school. We now stay in comfort at the River Club.

CHAPTER 23

Visiting The South

In 1990 May and I were invited to visit our friends Jim and Mary Greene at their condominium on Fripp Island, South Carolina. We were both taken with the island and pleased to have our winter cut short. We bought the condominium next door to the Greenes and started spending the month of March there. I was able to play tennis and row on the waterways next to the island. We made friends with Stef Meyer and his wife Kay, and I played backgammon with him.

Alligators frequented the marshes on the landward side of the island, which made tipping over in my shell a matter of considerable worry. I remember rowing past a beach one day and seeing a twelve-foot monster sunning himself. Another time my oar broke, and I tipped over. (Both oars are necessary to keep a single shell upright.) I was able to drag the boat into the reeds, tip it upright, put the broken part of the oar into the oarlock, and limp back to the landing dock without further adventure.

Our unit was the only one on the beach that had only one bedroom, which made it popular with renters. That, in turn, provided us with a modest rental income. By 1997 May was finding our unit too crowded for long stays, so we bought a house overlooking the marsh. I finally sold that house in 2006, when coping with it and its repairs became difficult to do from a distance.

CHAPTER 24

Backgammon

When I started playing backgammon at the Harvard Club, I set aside $200 and figured I would stop playing if I lost that amount. I kept the $200 in an envelope, adding my winning and subtracting my losses. The money grew in a very satisfactory fashion. Eventually I opened a brokerage account with my winnings and started investing the funds in the stock market. At its peak, the fund totaled $210,000. As a result of market slumps, it now stands at about $144,000. On my best night at the backgammon table I won $1,000. On my worst night I lost $600.

One day I was playing backgammon at the Harvard Club with a friend while I was waiting for Sheila to join me for dinner. Another man was watching and when my friend had to leave, I asked if he would like to play. I introduced myself and he asked if I was "one of the backgammon-playing Osbornes?" meaning my brother Richard and my son Christopher. I said I was. He said his name was Bill Roberti and I was instantly very nervous. Bill Roberti was, I knew, a professional backgammon player and one of the best in the world. We agreed on the stakes (five dollars a point). In the first game he doubled me, and I dropped. In the second game I, my hand shaking, doubled him. He dropped! At that moment Sheila appeared and she and I went to dinner. I was relieved to have come out even with a player as good as Roberti.

I had played backgammon in college with my classmate and friend Bruce MacIntyre. When I received an invitation from him to go to Huston and play in a tournament at his club, I jumped at the chance. The event was fun, and I managed to win a prize in the second flight.

May and I were going to fly up to Dallas for a cable convention after the tournament. Among the other players in the tournament was Sid Murchison, the oil baron. He and a group of

Dallas players had flown down from Dallas in his private plane for the tournament and Bruce arranged for us to fly with him to Dallas. The plane was large and comfortably fitted out. When we were nearing Dallas Sid asked me in a rather loud voice if he should tell the pilot to radio ahead for a taxi to meet May and me to drive us into town. He said there were no cabs in the portion of the field reserved for private planes. Overhearing his question several of the other passengers volunteered to give us a ride, which we accepted. I have always felt that Sid asked that question in precisely that fashion so that someone else would offer us a ride. I have always been grateful to him for his kindness.

CHAPTER 25

Osborne Association Board

After my Uncle Charles died in 1961, I took his place on the board of the Osborne Association (OA) The association had been founded by my grandfather as part of his effort to try to reform the American prison system. Austin McCormick, a protégé of TM, was head of the association and a leading light in prison reform. After his death his assistant, Robert Hannum had taken over his job. Unfortunately, Robert proved to be less than satisfactory. When I joined the board, we had three employees, one program and were indeed struggling. My cousin, Tom Osborne, suggested that we should consider shutting the organization down. I did not want to do that and when Bill Dean, who was on the OA board, suggested we should merge with the Correctional Association I was in favor of the step. We talked to them about terms and the idea was expressed that we simply turn over all our assets to them. I was opposed to this and suggested that we merge the boards of directors and have their executive director, Bob Gangi, run both organizations. This was approved by both boards, and we moved our operation to the Correctional Association's office on East 12th Street. Robert Hannum, who had been running the OA, left, and we hired Liz Gaynes to be our program director. When our board was discussing hiring Liz some members were concerned that her husband was in prison. I pointed out that we were hiring Liz, not her husband, and she was hired.

Liz was the turning point for the Osborne Association. She thought up new programs, found the funding for them and made sure that they succeeded. The programs were mostly successful, and we grew to be larger than the Correctional Association. Eventually it was decided that the Correctional and Osborne associations had different goals and should go their separate ways. The Correctional Association concentrated on prison inspections and made suggestions as to possible changes which might be made in the prison system. The Osborne Association was running programs to aid inmates and ex-inmates. Both executive directors were in favor of the step, so we went ahead with the plan. Osborne had grown substantially and has continued to grow. It now has a budget of forty-two million dollars and 350 employees.

The question came up about which board members should serve on which board. After considerable discussion I suggested that all board members should be appointed to both boards. Then those who did not wish to serve on one board or the other could simply resign from the less desired board. They could, I said, vote with their feet. This was approved and has worked very well. While most members chose one board or the other, some continued to serve on both boards. I served on the Osborne board for more than fifty years and watched it grow to be a force in the field of prison reform. I am very pleased that my children, Lucretia, Betsey, and Lithgow and my grandson Swift, are now or have been active in the association. Sheila and I went to a party in New York City and found that Martha Stewart, the media celebrity, was among the guests. She had done time in federal prison on a stock fraud charge, and I thought she might be interested in helping the association. When I suggested this to her she took one look at me, turned her back, and walked away.

CHAPTER 26

Osborne Memorial Association

The Osborne Memorial Association was started by my great-grandmother Eliza Wright Osborne, and my grandfather, Thomas Mott Osborne, in 1907 for the promotion of the moral and mental well-being of the working men and women of Auburn and Cayuga County and the literary work of the Woman's Educational and Industrial Union. The Association had a small portfolio and had been run by my Uncle Charles. He gave out funds whenever it suited him, mostly to the Woman's Union. There was also a fund donated by the Memorial Association and held by the Union as long as it continued its original purpose. When the Union joined forces with the YMCA it seemed to me that the Union was no longer serving its original purpose. We asked that the money be returned, and it was. I had expected some opposition, but there was none. Since then, the fund distribution has been by a board made up mostly of family members. I ran the association, managing the portfolio, filing the tax returns, and distributing the grants. Minturn is now taking over this duty.

In 2014 I decided that professional management would do a better job and we turned the fund over to the Central New York Community Foundation. They manage the portfolio and tell us how much money we have to give away each year. For a number of years, I would decide where the money should be spent, and the board would dutifully approve of my decisions. Then I got a better idea. Each of the five board members decides where one sixth of the income should go. The sixth share goes back into the fund so that it will grow in size. In my view having each member have the final say for a portion of the funds has worked very well. Some of the time I am not enthusiastic about some of the decisions that are made, but I still think it is a good arrangement. The board members think it is just fine. When we merged into the foundation our fund totaled $475,000. Currently, it is $704,000.

CHAPTER 27

Erik as an Athlete

Athletics has always been an important part of my life from my school days on. I played football, hockey, and lacrosse at Deerfield, enthusiastically but not particularly well, When I went to Harvard, I rowed in an eight-oared shell as an undergraduate and in a single shell as a graduate. When I came back to Auburn, I played squash in the winter and tennis in the summer. I enjoyed them both very much.

I played squash both at the Auburn YMCA and at the Racquet and Tennis Club in New York City. I found it a great form of exercise. One of my regular opponents was my very good friend Charlie Adams. One day when we came back to the changing room after playing, we found our mutual friend, George Iocolano, doing a headstand. He had become interested in yoga, hence the head stand. I had become mildly interested in yoga and had taught myself to do headstands. I had an idea. I started criticizing George for his performance, criticizing his stance. As I had hoped Charlie could not resist. He turned to me and said, "I bet you five dollars you cannot do that." I took his bet, did the headstand, and collected the five dollars.

One day I was at the Harvard Club in New York and in need of exercise. I went to the club's gym and found a rowing machine the like of which I had never seen before. I sat down and tried it and recalled how much I enjoyed rowing. After finishing my row, I went downstairs, called up Concept2, the maker, and ordered one of their machines. I used that machine more and more, and in 1997 I set a new World record for 2000 meters for men 70 years and older. In 2007 at the CRASH-B sprints I was able to set another world record eighty and over. I hasten to say that both records have since been broken. I continue to enjoy rowing on the machine, listening to audiobooks while I do so. I am sure rowing has helped to keep me in good health. My goal now is to set a new world record 100 and over.

I did not fare as well on the water as I did on the machines. I purchased an Alden Ocean shell in the 1980s and started competing in Alden races. Alden shells are broader in the beam and shorter than racing singles. They are slower but more stable and less likely to tip over. Racing singles, on the other hand, are very tippy. Any rower who tells you he has never tipped over in a racing single is probably a liar. Offhand I can remember tipping over four times.

After I had been competing in my Alden for a few years I decided to shift to racing singles in 1995 as there were more races to compete in and more people to compete against. The competition was almost entirely in head races where one started sequentially and rowed against the clock. The person with the lowest time is the winner. The racers were generally divided into age groups. Sometimes, however, the competition was with handicaps of a certain number of seconds subtracted depending on the rower's age. I rowed competitively from 1995 to 2013. My best showing was in 1999, a second place in a field of nineteen at the Head of the Charles in Boston. In 2013 I rowed in the Head of the Green in Putney, Vermont and rowed so slowly that I was passed by the first two competitors in the next race. I decided to make that my last race, as it was unfair to get in the way of other rowers. At 86 it seemed unlikely that I was going to be able to row any faster in the future. I have since stopped rowing on Owasco Lake in the racing shell as Sheila worries about my safety.

I only rowed in one 2,000-meter sprint race. That was in the World Masters Championships in Martindale, Canada in 2010. There were six 80-year-olds in the race: A Japanese, who was first; an Argentinian, who was second; a Brazilian, who was third; Erik, who was fourth; a Canadian, who was fifth, and another Yank, who was last. I remember thinking that the Japanese was probably in the Japanese army in World War II just as I was in the US Army.

CHAPTER 28

Our Children

When we married May was very anxious to have children and I went along with her even though I was still in graduate school. She was devastated when she had a miscarriage in the fall of 1950. After several trips to her gynecologist, he determined the miscarriage was caused by a cyst on one of her ovaries. He said the ovary needed to be removed. He removed the ovary in the spring of 1951. In June of 1953 Samuel Peabody Osborne arrived robust and healthy. May was thrilled. He was named after May's cousin and my former roommate. In the spring of 1954 May became pregnant again. At first everything was fine. Then in June May started to bleed and we feared she was going to lose the baby. After a race from Willow Point to the hospital, we were told the baby was alive, but that May needed to stay in bed until she could safely give birth. She stayed in bed, but things were not easy. I was working as a reporter and Sam and May needed attention. We hired a practical nurse and struggled as best we could. It was not easy. My mother helped from time to time. One day she gave Sam a bath. Afterwards she appeared from the bathroom shaken. She said it was the first time she had ever bathed a baby.

In November May was allowed out of bed and on November 7th, 1954, Christopher Raben-Levetzau Osborne arrived. He was healthy, but not as robust as Sam had been.

After Christopher we welcomed:
Sarah Sedgwick Osborne on December 11, 1955,
Elizabeth Endicott Osborne, June 1, 1957,
Lithgow Osborne II, May 9, 1959,
Minturn Sedgwick Osborne, October 8, 1960,
Lucretia Mott Osborne, July 21, 1962.

When Sam was told that Sally was due to arrive, he asked if, since we were getting a new baby, did we have to give the old one back. We told him that we would keep Christopher.

I was appointed to the board of directors of the National Bank of Auburn and served for many years. I enjoyed my time on the board and liked working with fellow board members. One of the features of the board service was that we received $35 in cash for attending the monthly meeting. Since this was extra money and in cash, I decided to share it with my children. I would give each child one dollar and take them to Nichols, a lower priced general merchandise store, so that they could spend the dollar. I decided that they should be allowed to make up their own minds and that I would let them take as long as they wished. They took a long time, going from aisle to aisle trying to decide. I thought that having them make up their own minds would be part of their education.

Another feature about my directorship which the children discovered was that they could overdraw their accounts without having the checks bounce. This was something which they apparently did quite regularly. I only learned this fact recently. In thinking about this bit of information it occurred to me that in all the time I had banked at the Auburn Trust Company, where my uncle was a director, the bank had never stopped payment on an overdrawn check. The first time such a thing happened to me was after I had opened an account at the Harvard Trust Company.

I remember being outraged and complaining to the bank and they being less than sympathetic. Since I was fourteen when I first had a checking account and twenty when I had opened an account at the Harvard Trust Company, I suspect there must have been overdrawn checks prior to that check. Could it be that Auburn Trust honored the checks because my uncle was a director? I will never know but I have my suspicions.

Neither May nor I were much impressed with the quality of the Auburn school system. We had both gone to private schools and felt that the children would get a far better education if they were to go to private schools too. Since there was no private school in Auburn, we decided we would have to send them to boarding schools. I have never counted how much I have spent on my children's and grandchildren's educations in school and college. However, I am sure it is well over a million dollars. I have always considered money well spent. The children all graduated successfully from boarding school. College was a different matter. All my children either dropped out of college or changed colleges at one time or another. They all went back and graduated successfully and, in the course of time, received graduate degrees. I think they had all concentrated, while in boarding school, on getting into college. When in college for a while they started to wonder why they were there and what the future would bring. This was when they dropped out or changed colleges.

Sam went to Indian Mountain, Holderness School and then to St. Lawrence University and has an MBA degree from Northeastern University. He now works for Braidio, an internet platform company, in their sales division. He is married to Eleanor Johnson. They have three sons, Frederik, Alexander, and Benjamin., and one grandson, Freddy. Christopher went to Indian Mountain School, Westminster School and then to Boston University, and Boston College Law School. He now works for Braidio as chief financial officer. He is married to Sandra Fulmer.

Sally went to Dana Hall School and to Tufts College. She retired in 2017 after teaching for 23 years at Nightingale-Bamford School in New York City. She currently works as a tutor.

She has two children, Valentine and Swift, and three granddaughters, Astrid, Ursula, and Jane. She is married to Robert V. Edgar.

Betsey went to St. Paul's School, Harvard College and has a Master of Fine Arts degree in Fiction Writing from Columbia University. She writes and is retired from teaching at Nightingale-Bamford School in New York City. She is married to Madelene Stein. She is the author of a novel *The Natural History of Uncas Metcalfe* and is writing another novel.

Lithgow went to the Rectory School, Westminster School, Sarah Lawrence College, and New York School of Interior Design and is married to Charles Burleigh. He works as a fine arts appraiser.

Minturn went to Groton School and Kenyon College and received a master's in administration from Syracuse University. He now works in sales for Exponential Power, an electronics battery controller systems company. He has three children, Rosemary, Lillie, and Worth.

Lucretia went to Groton School and Boston University and has advanced degrees from Portland State University and the University of Pennsylvania. She is married to Jonathon Wells. She runs her own consulting firm, dealing with the problems of private schools.

I feel that I have been very fortunate in that I have liked all the people my children and grandchildren have chosen as spouses. From time to time, I would tell some child who had erred that "he or she could be replaced by a machine that makes no noise." I did this until the day that Lucretia, about five at the time, asked "Daddy, where is the machine?" When I asked "What machine?" she said, in all earnestness, "The machine that makes no noise." I never made that statement again. Another time when my Aunt Janet came to Sunday lunch at Willow Point, I brought Lucretia, about four, to meet her. Janet said "Hullo Lucretia, I am your Great Aunt Janet" and Lucretia asked "What's so great about you?" Happily, Janet thought it was funny.

When Betsey and Minturn went off to boarding school Lucretia was left by herself and felt lonely. To help cheer her up in the winter I would take her out to Willow Point, and we would stand at the end of the point and shoot clay pigeons. One summer she worked for a law firm in Washington. The firm invited the summer interns to a picnic at a partner's country place. A feature of the picnic was clay pigeon shooting. Each male intern was given five shots, and they were not doing very well. Lucretia, who was clad in a two-piece bathing suit, decided she did not want to stand in line, so she went to the head of the line. The man running the shoot gave her a chance. She broke all five clay pigeons.

My son Christopher at one point in his life had a two-foot long boa constrictor as a pet. I could never figure out how snakes could be pets. But never mind that, he had one and I had to look after it when May took the children on their Western trip. The snake was kept in a wash tub with a screen on top. I did not have to feed him anything, as I recall. I just had to provide him with water, which I did. Later he escaped into the house and could not be found. May gathered the children about her and told them that the escaped snake was a family secret and should not be shared with the Waits next door. Years later I discovered a snake skeleton in the cellar under my office. I have always assumed it was Christopher's pet.

CHAPTER 29

My Children's Recollections

I am very proud of my children and have asked them to tell of their memories of particular events during their growing up years. What follows is their feedback:

Sam recalls:

My father ran the family newspaper for many years. One of his first tasks was to move the newspaper from its dusty, dirty, four-story building with a first floor dominated by an aging printing press, into a sleek modern building with a new printing press. Building a newspaper plant was unlike many businesses, where you just built the building with a nod to the equipment that was going into it. Building a newspaper had to start with the printing press, and you built the building around it. This was because the printing press was big, paper rolls that fed it were the size of large baby elephants, and where they were stored had to be waterproof.

(But that is a story for another day).

So, after the decision was made to build the building, the next step was a road trip to see other newspaper printing presses so that you could get a sense of what was needed to accommodate the largest and single most expensive piece of office equipment my father would ever own. I think the second was what I called the "largest Brownie camera in captivity". It was the camera used to take pictures of the mocked-up page so they could create the page that was used for printing the paper. My father planned a trip to three newspapers of a similar size to the *Citizen Advertiser*. My memory was a little vague, but I believe he planned to visit one newspaper a day with two overnight stays.

Then the best part came (at least for a 12-year-old boy who had just come home from boarding school) "Did you and Christopher want to go with me to see these printing presses?" I was thrilled when he added the "with me".

My memory is a little hazy after that, but what I do remember: eating steak for every meal, presents from the publishers from each of the newspapers, climbing on three of the biggest printing presses I had ever seen, but most of all spending one on one time with my father for three straight days.

My favorite memories growing up were the money meeting and Nichols, and swimming at the YMCA on Sunday afternoon. My father worked at the family-owned newspaper six days a week, so he was not around much during the day. He came home for lunch sometimes but was always there for dinner. (Imagine seven children eating together at once, being all chaotic and not getting much one-on-one with Dad).

My father was on the board of the National Bank of Auburn, where he lent his sage advice to the bank and other members of the board. For this sage advice, he was paid an undisclosed sum of money, some of which he kept for himself for wine, fast cars, and chocolate. (This is sheer speculation on my part and subject to my own bias—this is what I would have spent it on.) However, he did share with his children some of this largess. This is where Nichols comes in.

Nichols was the forerunner of the popular Dollar Stores that dot the rural American landscape. Nichols was located in a far corner of a mall in a far corner of Auburn. My father would load us into the family station wagon and off we would go for an evening of retail adventuring. Once we arrived at the far corner of the mall in the far corner of Auburn, my father would hand out a portion of what became known as the "Money Meeting" money. We were let loose in the store. Seven of us roamed the aisles looking for that one thing that would delight and entrance us for at least five minutes on the ride home. My father would sit quietly in the store or roam the aisles patiently answering questions on cost, and durability, as well as offering his sage advice on our potential purchases. Once the shelves had been completely reviewed and analyzed, booty in hand, and the money meeting money spent, we were off to home.

For some reason, no one used the YMCA pool much on Sunday afternoon, so like Nichols, we had it all to ourselves. My father did not swim but answered all our various questions, kept an eye out for any possible drownings, and waited patiently as we exhausted ourselves. We would arrive home with wet hair smelling of chlorine, to find my mother happy to see us. It was only later when I was older, and my Sundays were taken up with other things, that it occurred to me that these Sundays served two purposes, giving my mother a well-deserved break and my brothers and sisters alone time with my father.

I do not remember the year, but it was definitely one of the first three I spent at a pre-boarding school in Lakeville, CT called Indian Mountain School. I was sent off to IMS because my grades at the local public school were less than stellar and my parents had the confidence that the Doolittles who were headmaster and mistress of the school and long-time friends of my parents, could make a much-needed mid-course correction of my academics. The school was very typical of Grade 1-8 private schools in those days. They seem to be clustered tightly in the tri-state area of CT, MA, and New York. Most students that went to school there were day students from the surrounding area. The boarding students (all boys) came from New York City (the upper parts), Southern CT, Massachusetts, Maryland, and other enclaves of the wealthy and highly placed. I was born and lived in Auburn, NY and IMS represented the first time away from home for any length of time. Because the school days were highly scheduled and regimented, I looked forward to vacations. The night before vacation was always a period of wind down for the boarding students. The day students had deserted us and gone home. Dinner was typical fare, and unlike other days there was no real after-dinner activity (study hall, work crew, etc.). So, a bunch of us were doing something we never had a chance to do—just hanging out.

The subject of "What are you doing for vacation?" came up. Grant went first, "My Mom is taking me to New York to see her sister. I think my dad is working." Kevin said, "I am going skiing out west with my little brother." Rob said, "My parents are taking me to England." John said, "I am going home to Boston, but all my friends don't have vacation until after I come back here." I am sitting here thinking this is all cool: New York, skiing, England or time alone to watch the programs I wanted to.

Then my turn came: "Osborne what are you doing?" "I am going home to Auburn, NY." "Will your parents be there?" Me, ducking my head to hide my embarrassment. (What can I say. I am not going to Europe) "Yeah and my brothers and sisters." How many brothers and sisters do you have?' "Six. three brothers and three sisters" "Wow, do you all hang out together." "Yeah, we play baseball, and kickball, my dad takes us swimming at the Y, if the weather is nice, we go to our place at the lake, we eat dinner together (suddenly remembering what an awful cook my mother was, but they did not need to know that), watch TV together. "So, your parents do not make you go to museums, libraries or force you to hang out with your brothers and sisters." "Oh, we go to the local library, my mom lets us take out any books we want."

The universal reaction to my answers was "That is so cool." I realized at that moment that the important stuff was not what I was doing for Spring vacation but who I was doing it with.

Christopher recalls:

Among my friends my father is considered a quiet, even-tempered man. When I was younger and in public school in the 5th grade, my report cards accurately reflected my ability as a student. I was large for my age and that was probably the only reason I was passed on to the 3rd, 4th and finally 5th grade. My brother Sam, although a better student than I, also faced the same predicament in that his apparent intelligence was not reflected in his scholarly work. My parents decided to seek medical advice as to why we were failing so miserably (our dyslexia had not yet been diagnosed). The four of us went to an institution in Syracuse where Sam and I underwent a battery of tests: audio, visual, mental, and psychological. Apparently, the doctors determined there was nothing wrong with our eyesight, hearing, or mental ability. They (there were three doctors, all in white coats) called the four of us into a conference room and revealed that the reason that Sam and I received such terrible grades was that we were mad at our parents. Until that time, I had never seen my father get angry.

What I remember was his standing up and

speaking in a measured tone to the doctors and even at that time it was clear to me that there was volcanic rage beneath his words. I cannot express how shocking it was. I knew he loved me, and I knew that he did not think the grades I received reflected my intelligence, but it was such a bald show of faith and love that the memory of that day (including the silent ride home) will be with me forever.

Here is a more recent story about my father. This last summer Sandra and I were at Willow Point, and we were playing Scrabble with my cousin Lisa, the daughter of my Uncle Devens. As was my wont, I was riding Lisa pretty hard about her low score. When my father came into the room, Lisa asked, "Uncle Erik, why is your son so mean?" My father, without pausing, said, "He gets it from his Uncle Devens."

Sally recalls:
Three meals a day for seven children and two adults.
Breakfast: Eggs, toast, sometimes cereal, orange juice, milk, occasionally coffee cake. instant coffee and decaf for adult.
Lunch: Peanut butter and jelly, marmalade and (sometimes Fluff) or datenut bread from a can

with cream cheese or grilled cheese squished with a can whilst cooking.

Dinner: crock pot inventions—lentils, chili, sloppy joes. Or roasted chicken, Brussel sprouts, spinach cooked with a can of mushroom soup.

Snacks: Spam fried with maple syrup, and toast, toast, toast,

Once a week: Carroll's hamburgers, Kentucky Fried Chicken or MacDonald's Milk on tap, eggs almost straight from the chicken, no processed meats, no plastic wrap only wax paper, no iceberg lettuce, no grapes—we were ahead of our time!

We learned to make our own eggs early on thanks to the egg cooker, cookies thanks to slice and bake, sandwiches because we 'knew' how to make them better. Not everything was eaten by the seven of us—dried yeast was untouched and the can of clams with shells included. I still like eating with lots of people no matter what food is served.

Betsey recalls:

I was in my early 20s, driving home alone in the car my mother called "the Silver Ghost," on the ramp of Exit 40 in Weedsport, approaching the toll booth. The drive I took most often in those days—maybe just after college—was from Boston to Auburn and back again, but I'm not sure where I was coming from on this trip. As I approached the exit, I glanced away for a second to look for my wallet. I leaned to the right, feeling in the well. What I remember most about the crash is the absoluteness of being stopped. There was no give. Of being on passenger's side, wondering if my wallet had slipped under the seat. Probably, I wasn't going all that quickly, maybe 10 or 15 miles an hour, but I can't be sure.

I wasn't a great driver, but I've always been one for pumping the brakes, so I had probably slowed down as I came off the ramp. The next thing I remember is looking along with the other driver at the bumper of his 18-wheeler truck that was already in line at the booth. Not a scratch on it. The front of the station wagon, my parents' station wagon, was badly dented, but I was able to drive it. And so, I drove it home, and parked it in the garage. When my father came back from work, I told him what had happened, and we went to look at the damage. The headlights still worked! I knew that somehow; I'd gotten away with something and of course it could have been much worse. "I'll call Charlie Adams in the morning," my father said. (Mr. Adams handled my parents' insurance.) We had dinner, and he announced he was going back to work. At least the car was drivable was the feeling I think we both had. He left and probably I settled into the sunroom to watch television. Strangely, I don't think anyone else was around, which was very unusual. I can count on two hands the number of times I remember being alone with my father in 65 years. He came back inside and asked me to come see something. We both laughed at the headlights of the car pointing up crazily into the sky. I could tell you many more stories about breaking things—from a lightbulb that exploded when hit with a tennis ball to a vase made by my grand-mother—but none of these touched off anger or even irritation (well, maybe once) in either of my parents, who seemed to share the idea that their children weren't breaking things on purpose. I always felt that trust and the idea that we, my six siblings and I, counted more than objects.

Lithgow recalls:

I guess one of the most vivid memories I have of growing up is a visit to Willow Point during the winter. I might have been nine or ten years old. It was decided that we would walk across the lake to Dolphin Point and back again. I know that we made the trip alone, but I have no idea if we were alone at Willow Point. It seems unlikely that we would be alone, but I cannot remember whether there were others. I remember this because he and I were hardly ever alone together. There were always others.

We stood at the shore looking east across the vast frozen lake. I was thrilled at the prospect of walking on the ice and being in the middle of the lake. It was very cold and silent, with only a bit of wind. The surface was a bit rough from snow, but there were patches of ice, so I walked carefully. As we made our way, I began to ask the inevitable questions about how thick the ice was and how cold it had to be to be safe to walk on. He always seemed to know the answers.

As we approached the middle of the lake, we began to hear the ice creaking and cracking. His calm gave me confidence and we kept walking. We were more than halfway across when there was a very long, loud cracking noise. We stopped, silently staring ahead. I looked around to see if there was any change in the surface of the frozen lake, any evidence to indicate that we might be in trouble. I had no voice to express my rising fear. The terror of crashing through the ice seemed very real. I could only think of the characters I saw in movies or read about in books where they met their doom engulfed in freezing waters.

As ever, he remained calm and voiced no concern. Wordlessly, slowly, he reached down and took my hand. In an instant I was calm. Every terrifying mage that passed through my head disappeared. We walked the rest of the way in silence.

Minturn recalls:

I must have been either 9 or 10 years old and I had just come back to Willow Point from summer camp outside of Buffalo. While I was at the camp, I was taught how to sail a little sunfish on the pond at the camp and I felt quite proficient with my nautical skills. Dad suggested that he and I go out in the two sailboats and sail around, which was great for me because there was so much I wanted to teach him about sailing. I don't know if anyone remembers but we had two sailboats at one point. One was some kind of sailfish, and the other was this blue boat with a kind of catamaran wannabe construction whereby it had two prows in the front and in the back as opposed to one single prow. Anyway, Dad rigged his boat, and I rigged mine. It was not a really windy day but there was a breeze and as we pushed off, my sail was hit by a stronger wind which began to push me farther and farther down the lake. I looked at the size of the sail, I looked at the size of the boat and I looked at the size of the lake and I realized that I was way out of my depth. I started to panic and cry. I shouted (screamed?) to Dad who seemed miles away and he yelled out to just drop everything; He was coming to get me. I dropped the tiller and the main sheet as if they were hot metal, and the wind pushed me around to the place where it could do the least damage other than gently push me down the lake. Anyway, Dad came out to me really quickly and pulled up alongside. He told me to grab the rope in the front of my boat and climb into the sailfish. Once I was in, he sailed us back to the beach where we left the slower boat and took off in the one I had been on.

I'll never forget how calm he was in the light of my panic. I know that at the time I felt I was at risk of drowning; the fact of the matter was that the wind would have pushed me to one shore or another and I would have been found. It certainly would have been search and rescue and not search and recovery.

Anyway, we went out and the wind picked up, it turned out to be a pretty brisk sail and we made it across the lake quickly. We turned North and started sailing along the far side of the lake. About 15 yards or 20 yards ahead of us there was the remainder of a concrete dock sticking out of the water. It was just one post maybe five or six inches above the water line and, as I was sitting in the front of the boat, I pointed it out to Dad and told him that we were heading right for it. He just nodded and kept looking off in the distance.

He didn't change tack or anything and just kept on going straight for it. I didn't want to say anything but finally I said, "Dad! It is right in from of us!" and he nodded and did not say anything. We kept bearing down on the post until the very last minute he pushed the tiller and steered by the post with literally inches to spare. I turned to watch it go by along the side of the boat and I looked up at Dad. He had this huge grin on his face continuing to look off at the horizon and I'll never forget how happy he looked. It is the image I have of him in my mind's eye whenever I think about how much I love him.

Lucretia recalls:
When asked to write one memory of Dad, I am brought to a standstill. I want the memory to reflect a time with Dad that captures all that he is to me, and that has simply proved impossible. I had a chance to read some of my siblings' reflections and a thread that runs through these memories is the appreciation of the moments we had Dad to ourselves. This rare opportunity resonates with me, and I am reminded of the year I was home alone with Mom and Dad. Minturn and Betsey went off to boarding school in the Fall which left Grover St. to Mom, Dad, and me. I was 12 years old and had never imagined them all to myself.

One thing that stands out for me is playing squash, going for runs, shooting clay pigeons at Willow Point, or doing yardwork with Dad. We had these times together and I cherished the opportunity to either talk or be silent. Peppered in our talking where games Dad would create to pass our time, counting one-one thousand, two-one thousand at each highway marker between cars... never closer than the count of five, the knot that includes the rabbit coming out of the hole, going around the tree, and then back into the hole (a bowline), or some such course of action to bundle the sticks before putting them at curbside. When we played squash, he would start down negative 10 and we both viewed a close game as a victory.

If I borrowed money, I had to give him something important to me to serve as a guarantee that I would pay back the debt. That summer I broke my ankle, and he used a piece of wood and some rope to secure my cast on the pedal of the stationary bicycle. Once I could run again, he paid for my new running sneakers after I had logged a hundred miles. In retrospect, the time together with my father and the care and attention to what we shared, without too much conversation, made me feel special in a pool of seven.

I know this was like my siblings, all of whom he adored.

CHAPTER 30

Life with May

May and I, coming as we did from remarkably similar backgrounds, had very similar points of view. This led to our having a very happy life together. We rarely disagreed about how to raise our children. If we did have a disagreement, we would sort it out in advance so that we could always present a united front in dealing with the children. We never had any disagreements about major decisions in our marriage. May was happy to leave Boston and come to Auburn. She was happy in Auburn and enjoyed her friends here and her work in the community. She particularly liked being head of the Auburn Housing Authority and being on the

Seymour Library board. She was happy to have me work at the newspaper and agreed with my selling both the newspaper and cable. I was perfectly happy to vacation in Murray Bay.

May took the last agonizing years of her life very bravely. She rarely complained as the cancer continued to grow and managed to put on a cheerful front in the face of every bit of bad news. Even in her very last hours on her death bed in 1999 she never lost her sense of humor. When she became sicker it became clear that she had to go to the hospital. Before she went to the hospital for that last time, she had lost control of her bowels. I had helped her clean up and as she lay in bed, she lost control again. In vexation she said, "oh shit" and then, after a moment's pause, she added "and that's exactly what it is." She was taken to the hospital by ambulance soon after. The ambulance was halted by an auto wreck on the Fripp Island bridge. As a result, a helicopter was summoned to take her the rest of the way to the hospital. She died during the night. While we had both known for some time that the cancer was fatal, her loss still left a huge gap in my life. We had been married for more than forty-eight years. Calling up the children was very painful.

May left me a note which read:

Darling Erik,

I have loved you with every molecule I have. I hate to leave the party so soon. Together we have shared love, laughter, wonderful children. There never was a better husband and father and grandfather. I do believe in a future life together through all eternity. Always, my love, I believe we will be together again in eternity. I cannot bear it otherwise.
Your Maisie

Betsey had come down to see us and she and I flew back to Auburn with May's ashes for the funeral. After the funeral I can remember the sinking feeling when the children drove down the driveway and I was left alone and lonely in the Grover Street house.

CHAPTER 31
Life Afterwards

I tried to cope with the situation but without much success. My friends were all happily married, with their own lives to lead. Then I went to a cocktail party at Jean Metcalf Chapman's home. Sheila Vorreuter was there, but not with Donald O'Brien, the man I knew she had been seeing regularly. I invited her to join me for dinner and she accepted. I was much taken by her, and we had a very pleasant evening.

I continued seeing her and enjoying her company. As a result, I tried to find out if she was still seeing Donald. Nobody seemed to know or be particularly interested in my question. When it became apparent that her relationship with Donald O'Brien had ended, I became more and more interested.

When I went up to Murray Bay by myself during the summer of 2001, I found myself spending a great deal of time on the telephone with Sheila. I was missing her very much. We continued seeing each other and enjoying each other's company, drawing closer and closer together, and then falling in love.

We went to Murray Bay together the next year and, while there, decided to get married. We did so on September 21st, thus starting a very happy period of my life, which continues to this day.

I sometimes refer to Sheila as "the head nurse" for along with her love and devotion comes a determination to make sure that I take good care of myself. She is very firm when it comes to taking pills, using my cane, or driving the car.

She permitted day-time trips to and around Auburn but banned driving at night and trips out of town. (I did manage a drive to Skaneateles to get my car inspected.) While I was sometimes restive about her ukases I tried not to complain too much. I knew she issued them because she loves me, and I love her more for what she is and does. At the age of 97 while driving into town I went through a "Stop" sign because my mind was on something else. Happily, there were no other cars around so there was no accident. But I was worried that there could have been an accident, so I gave up driving. Sheila and my children had been highly critical of my driving. (Betsey had gone so far as to decline to drive with me.) They were all very pleased with my decision. Now I cadge rides from Sheila, Chris Kahl, or my friends.

Sheila has worked hard to bring both Willow Point and Grover Street to her very high standards and has succeeded very well. The gardens at Willow Point overflow with a profusion of blooms that take your breath away. They have never looked so beautiful. The vistas down and across the lake are a delight, as is the view up the glen. The inside of the house is handsomely furnished and very comfortable. I am always proud to show it to visitors.

The Grover Street house also benefits from Sheila's energy and ideas. When Sheila sold her house, she brought some of her furniture and pictures to Grover Street, to add to its comfort and style. She has also worked hard on the garden there with great success. Sitting in our back garden it is hard to believe one isn't in the country.

In addition to her furniture and pictures, Sheila brought her two dogs, Lilly and Bear, whom I enjoyed very much. They took to their new homes with enthusiasm. Bear would patrol the whole of the Point every morning and bark at any boats that he deemed to be too close to our shore.

May had been always interested in making housework easier and decided that an artificial Christmas tree would work better than a real one. As a result, we purchased an artificial one, which we used for several years. After May died, I did not use the tree for several years. as Sheila, an ardent gardener, did not approve of things artificial. Finally, when I needed the space, I decided to dispose of the tree. At first, I was going to put it out with the trash. Then I had a better idea. I set the tree up against the back fence and waited. I waited for six months. Finally, Sheila came storming into the house and announced that someone had put a fake tree in the backyard. It was then that I put the tree into the trash.

Sheila has brought peace and contentment to my declining years for which I am most grateful. I consider that I have been more fortunate than anyone could dare wish. We decided that the apartment in New York and the house in Fripp Island involved too much traveling, so we sold them both. (At a modest profit I am happy to say.)

Now, at the age of 97, we live in Grover Street in the winter and move to Willow Point in the summer and enjoy visits from our children, grandchildren, and great-grandchildren. We live quietly, going out to dinner at restaurants and eating at home the rest of the time. We entertain occasionally. I work at my computer most days, answering emails, paying bills, keeping track of my portfolio and writing. I also play bridge twice a week and poker once a week. I row on my Concept2 machine six days a week, listening to audio books while I row. Beau, our amiable Labrador retriever, keeps us company and follows Sheila wherever she goes.

CHAPTER 32
Family Stories

TM at the Ritz

In 1910 my grandfather, TM, took an automobile tour of Europe with his sons David and Charles, two of their friends and a chauffeur. TM always believed in dressing suitably for the occupation in which he was engaged. As a result, he arrived at the Ritz in Paris dressed in a white cover-all, known as a "duster", which came with a white cover for his hat. It was designed to ward off the dust of unpaved roads. When he arrived at the front desk, he announced that he had a reservation. The clerk took one look at him and said there was no reservation under that name. TM's sons persuaded him to exchange his costume for his Chesterfield overcoat and Hamburg hat. He did so with great reluctance after a heated argument with his sons. When he went into the Ritz again the clerk told him that his rooms awaited him.

My Father in Norway

Below is a letter to me from my father when he was in Oslo as American ambassador to Norway.

Christmas Eve 1945

Dear Erik,

I'm feeling rather upset about you because I have wired all the rest of the family but have not got your address. I should have got it Saturday before I left the office. The trouble is I went home at noon and yesterday was Sunday and today the office was also closed, and I could only get your address by routing out Miss Sluchan and making her go down to the office and get it for me; and as she is temperamental as hell these days and considers herself very much "put upon" I hesitate to do that.

No one invited us for this evening, for which I am rather glad because then I can make it pretty much like any other evening.

Mr. Greene will be here for supper but is going out afterwards. I planned to have the Embassy party for the staff tonight but found out that the servants here at the house felt badly about that as Christmas Eve is the big occasion for all Norwegians; Christmas Day is not so important. So, as I didn't see that it made much difference to us, we had the Embassy affair on Sat. evening. I had hoped we could join with the British and put on some sort of a show. My chief idea was to keep my boys and girls from being too homesick by having some sort of communal enterprise which they could rehearse and plan for. So, I circulated a questionnaire to discover whether they could sing, dance, act or do parlor tricks. I drew an almost complete blank from the whole 70-odd! A less talented outfit one could hardly imagine. Finally, I bethought myself of some carol singing as there were one or two who said they had sung in choirs. So, we had rehearsals here three times last week with drinks and light refreshments. About 25 or 30 turned out and before Mr. Greene got through with them, they were pretty darn good. Mr. G. plays the piano and knows a great deal about music and has actually led orchestras. He was very lukewarm at first but before he got through, I could hardly restrain him—kept adding on new numbers and insisting that they sing three or four verses instead of one or two—as I suggested with a view to our time schedule and their voices. The rank and file also got very pepped up and I was sorry afterwards that I had not arranged for an appearance in the Palace courtyard, as I probably could have done, if I had thought of it in time. I didn't, for one reason because at the first rehearsal they were perfectly frightful, and Greene and I agreed that we couldn't take them anywhere. At the second rehearsal, they really got going and I thereupon plucked up heart to arrange for appearances outside the Soviet, French and British Embassies. I had a very diverting call upon my Russian colleague who doesn't speak much English and who was waiting for me with an interpreter, convinced, I am sure, that I was coming on high matters of state. It took him a little while to discover what it was all about but then he seemed very pleased; and on Sat. evening when we appeared he had his whole staff on hand, invited us in and fed us Russian cheese, Russian brandy and Russian wine and we departed singing "For he's a Jolly good fellow."

We had forgathered here at 5 for a final rehearsal and a cocktail. I had wanted to provide the singers with several cocktails, but Mr. Greene protested so violently that more than one small one would produce "whiskey voices" that I desisted. While the singers were practicing, five of the Embassy children (there are now a total of 8) were viewing the Christmas tree, opening their presents, and having their supper.

After the Soviet Embassy, we walked a hundred yards down the street to the French. There is very little staff there, but the Ambassador has quite a family including three young children. He also invited us in (although I had told him he mustn't) and fed us champagne. Then on to the British which was our final appearance. Our program had been: "Joy to the World "Hark the Herald Angels" "Silent Night" "It came upon a Midnight Clear" and "Jingle Bells"—not that the last is strictly speaking a carol but they sang it with such vigor that Greene—to my surprise—added it. At the British appearance we also sang "God Save the King" and "Star Spangled Banner." There was a staff party going on there—which we joined and drank mulled wine. (By this time, I had decided Greene had been quite correct on the cocktail issue.)

Supper here was at 9:30. A few people had gone off skiing or were celebrating with relatives, so we were "only" about 65. Food on the big table in the center and self-service but a place for everyone. There was an engagement to announce—Miss Helen Janeway, whose pa is a Brig. Gen. and her boss Lt. Lee Price who came over here with OSS and is now attached to the Embassy. Both are very nice young people. (As a matter of fact, she came over with Ma and me a year ago on the boat to England.)

The rest of the evening consisted of informal singing and dancing to a victrola. The whole business was, I think, a great success. Tomorrow, I go to lunch with the Nielsens and to dine with the Dutch Minister.

I watch the newspapers eagerly these days as to sunrise and sunset. Our day now is 7 minutes short of 6 hours. Today the sun rose at 9:30 and set (though no one saw it) at 3:13. I had never realized before that sunrise for a few days after Dec. 21 goes on getting later and later even though the day gets a little longer.

However, it is not as bad as it sounds because

there is a very long twilight, and it begins to get light shortly after eight. We had one large fall of snow and then a thaw which took most of it away. Now it has frozen again and the side streets and roads outside town are pretty slippery--although they put on a good deal of sand. It's years since I've been in a place where tire chains are considered part of usual winter equipment for a car, as they used to be with us. The next snow we get will probably stay with us the rest of the winter because thaws are not usual here. The sun never gets high enough to do any real business.

At noon it is only Just above the roof-tops and shadows in the middle of the day are long like evening shadows with us.

There is no use repining that we are not together. We are all, on the whole, very, very lucky. I hope you are not having too dismal a Christmas. I haven't heard from you for some time. I am anxious to hear about your new assignment. I am still in much doubt—based on Ma's letters—as to what is apt to happen to you.

With much love, your Pa.

My Parents' Wedding Announcement

Lillie Raben-Levetzau Weds Secretary
of American Legation, Son of
Ex-Warden Osborne

New York Times March 15, 1918

COPENHAGEN, Tuesday, March 12–
Coucntess Lillie Raben-Levetzau, daughter of the former Danish Minister of Foreign Affairs, was married today to Lithgow Osborne of New York, Secretary of the American Legation here. The bride's mother was Miss Nina Moulton of Boston.

The marriage was celebrated at Castle Aalholm, the estate of Count Raben-Levetzau, and was attended by 100 American and Danish guests. Cleveland Perkins of Washington was best man.

After the ceremony dinner was served in the great hall of knights of the castle. The King and Queen of Denmark sent a large porcelain lamp and a telegram of congratulation. Dowager Queen Louise and Prince Valdemar sent a large silver tea tray. There were also presents from Prince Gustavus and Princess Ingeborg of Sweden. Mr. and Mrs. Osborne will spend their honeymoon at Lekkende, an estate of Count Raben–Levetzau.

Mr. Osborne is a son of Thomas Mott Osborne, former Warden of Sing Sing, and he was a member of Ambassador James W. Gerard's staff in Berlin until the relations between this country and Germany were broken.

His bride is a well-known sculptress in Scandinavia. She is a granddaughter of the late Charles Moulton of Boston. The engagement was announced in December last.

Answers to the Clues on Page 116:
- Priscilla Mullins who married John Alden
- Rowing Machine
- Willow Point Silhouette Sign designed by LRLO.
- RAFT
- Tennis Court
- The Electric Generator

Editor's Note:

Upon fact-checking the Children's Recollections, it was noted that Christopher's trouncing of Lisa in Scrabble had much to do with Sandra and Christopher's recent memorization of the 107 acceptable 2-letter words listed in the Official Scrabble Players Dictionary (they were retired, for heavens' sake).

And upon further review, Lisa was questioned about her father Devens' influence on Christopher. She states that not only was he never a mean-spirited individual, even at his most competitive, but she remembers him as someone who never raised his voice or got particularly angry.

Like his younger brother, Erik.